Marjorie Cayg...

The British Museum 250 Years

THE BRITISH MUSEUM PRESS

Preface

London 1753. The most populous city in Europe. The richest city in Europe. The greatest financial centre in the world. A cosmopolitan place, where Voltaire had discovered the true meaning of political and intellectual freedom, where Handel had discovered himself as the master of the oratorio, and where Canaletto painted the Thames and made it as seductively glamorous as the Grand Canal. The London of Garrick and Reynolds, Hogarth and Doctor Johnson. The London in which the first national museum in the world was founded.

This book, written by the scholar-historian Marjorie Caygill, tells the story of an extraordinary experiment in public education. The Europe of 1753 was rich in collections of paintings and antiquities, books and natural curiosities. But they were overwhelmingly collections belonging to princes, prelates or noblemen, graciously opened to the public. The British Museum on the other hand was a startlingly new idea: a collection bought by Parliament that was to belong not to the king, nor to the state, but to every person in the land. It was to be not so much a public museum as a private museum of every citizen, a key instrument in achieving the Enlightenment dream of an informed and educated political community.

The idea that this collection should belong to everybody was given legal form by borrowing a structure from English family law, the trust. The point of a trust is to ensure that property is managed not just for the benefit of this generation, but is preserved also for the enjoyment of generations not yet born. This was always a venture aimed at posterity. And to show that the beneficiaries of this particular trust were the entire nation, three principal trustees were appointed – the Archbishop of Canterbury, the Lord Chancellor and the Speaker of the House of Commons, the leaders of the three component elements of Parliament. There had never been anything like it before, but the Trustee Museum, on the lines of the British Museum, was in succeeding generations to become the model for the whole English-speaking world.

The collection bought by Parliament in 1753, although then one of the most important anywhere in Europe, has been completely dwarfed by the acquisitions of the following 250 years. Marjorie Caygill traces the history of that expansion, the fruit of scholarship and wealth, of political power allied to connoisseurship and systematic collecting. The result is a collection unique in the world, where the cultures of all humanity from the earliest times to the present day can be studied under one roof. And this is still, as it was in the beginning, free to anybody who wants to enter it – truly a museum of the world, for the world.

It was one of the great dreams of the eighteenth century to gather objects from all corners of the globe and then to organise them in systematic categories, so that points of similarity and difference would emerge and the great scheme of the natural law would become clear. It was an ambition which in France took the published form of the *Encyclopédie*. In London, it was built as the British Museum.

That eighteenth-century ideal is now visited by 4.5 million people from all over the world every year. And it is an ideal which is surely more important now than it ever has been. As the world becomes more interdependent and more tightly linked, it is more and more essential to have a place where the interlocking stories of humanity can be seen and explored.

Neil MacGregor
Director
The British Museum

Old and new.
Head of the Egyptian
pharaoh Amenhotep III
(1390–1352 BC),
and the steel and glass
roof of the Queen
Elizabeth II Great Court.

Celebrating 250 Years

'Books for Mead and butterflies for Sloane' quipped the poet Alexander Pope in his 1731 satire on those who laid out their fortunes on 'drawings and designs', 'statues, dirty gods and coins' and 'monkish manuscripts'. This was the 'Age of the Enlightenment' when collectors might contemplate capturing in one place specimens of all the works of humanity and nature; and the museum of the physician and naturalist Sir Hans Sloane (1660–1753) was perhaps the finest of them all.

The origins of the British Museum lie in Sloane's will. Trained as a physician, in 1687 Sloane travelled to the West Indies whence he returned with an extensive natural history collection and established a lucrative medical practice at Nos 3 and 4 Bloomsbury Place, promoting a milk chocolate drink and making a fortune out of the sale of quinine. There too he indulged his universal collecting passion. In 1742, to the alarm of his family, he retired to his damp manor house by the river at Chelsea. Lacking an heir who shared his collecting mania he bequeathed his beloved collection to the British nation in return for £20,000 for his two daughters.

Sloane died on 11 January 1753, leaving an estimated 71,000 objects of all kinds, 50,000 books, manuscripts, prints and drawings, and 337 volumes of dried plants. Horace Walpole, a trustee of his will, sarcastically remarked on 'sharks with one ear and spiders as big as geese'. But the nation had acquired a bargain and, after negotiations with Parliament, Sloane's trustees agreed to relinquish control to a new institution, the first of a particular kind of museum which has since had many imitators – national, secular and freely open to the public.

On 7 June 1753 King George II, sitting in state in the House of Lords, gave his formal assent to an Act of Parliament which established the British Museum. Parliament, with evident relief, changed its nature by adding the hitherto neglected Cottonian collection of coins and manuscripts, given to the nation in 1700, and authorised the purchase for £10,000 of the Harleian manuscripts. The fourth founding collection was the Old Royal Library, given by King George II in 1757, which brought with it the right to a copy of every publication printed in the country and hence indefinite expansion.

The Museum's exhibition galleries and a reading room opened to the public on 15 January 1759, in 17th-century Montagu House in Bloomsbury, on the site where the British Museum remains today. At first visitors were drawn by the natural history collections – glittering and bizarre, scholarly and scientific. Antiquities and ethnography were relatively meagre, but in due course the balance began to change. From the voyages of Captain Cook, almost equivalent to today's expeditions into space, came ethnographical and natural history specimens never before seen in Europe. This was also the era of the Grand Tour: Classical antiquities began to permeate the collections, and in 1772 the purchase of the collection of Sir William Hamilton, particularly rich in Greek vases, gave the Museum its first antiquities of note. Other connoisseurs such as Mordaunt Cracherode, whose bequest of 1799 included an outstanding collection of prints and drawings, enriched the Museum.

Although admiration for the Classical collections held sway, the transformation of the Egyptian collection began in 1802 with the acquisition of the Rosetta Stone and other antiquities found by Napoleon's army in Egypt. If not quite 'art', their fascination began to take hold. From 1818 onwards colossal sculpture acquired by Henry Salt, then British Consul-General in Egypt, awed the public and, encouraged by the decipherment of the Rosetta Stone by Champollion in 1822, knowledge of this ancient culture began to emerge.

In 1816 came the so-called 'Elgin marbles', sold to the government by Lord Elgin. These included some of the sculptures of the Parthenon and other monuments in Athens, acquired by Elgin's artists and moulders, horrified at their continuing destruction. The Museum was active elsewhere in the Ottoman Empire and later sought out remains of Lykian Tombs (1840s), the Mausoleum of Halikarnassos (1850s) and the Temple of Artemis at Ephesos (1860s).

The Assyrians were known to the Victorians from the Bible but their cities were lost. In the 1840s and 1850s the Museum financed excavations by A.H. Layard and others. While prizing the magnificent sculptures, of equal interest to the Museum's curators was the discovery of Ashurbanipal's great library of cuneiform tablets, which made the Museum a focus for Assyrian studies and the decipherment of these ancient texts. Excavations continued throughout the 19th and into the 20th and 21st centuries.

Until the mid-19th century the Museum's horizons were relatively limited, but with the appointment to the staff of Augustus Wollaston Franks in 1851 the Museum began for the first time systematically to collect British and medieval European material, and prehistory, branched out into the Orient, and diversified its holdings of ethnography. Franks, perhaps the Museum's greatest benefactor, had a private fortune. He was one of a circle of major collectors whose collections, with tactful and determined urging, eventually came to the Museum. Franks himself in 1897 bequeathed 3,300 finger rings, 153 drinking vessels, 512 pieces of continental porcelain, 1,500 netsuke, 850 inro, over 30,000 bookplates, and miscellaneous items of jewellery and plate, among them the Oxus treasure, having already given around 7,000 objects.

The Museum did not remain as the founders first envisaged but it put out some sturdy offshoots. The first major break in the collections – the transfer of oil paintings – came with the establishment of a separate National Gallery in 1824 and subsequently the development of the National Portrait Gallery. Because of the pressure on space, the natural history collections were transferred to South Kensington in the 1880s, to become the Natural History Museum. Around a century later, in 1973, the library departments split off to form, with other libraries, a new institution – the British Library. In 1998 the British Library's new building at St Pancras was opened.

An integral part of the Museum is the public – at first somewhat grudgingly and now enthusiastically admitted. The Museum has been open to visitors since 1759 and, apart from three months in 1974, general admission has always been free. The early Trustees were torn between a responsibility to admit visitors as directed by Parliament and alarm at the well-deserved reputation for mayhem of the London mob. They solved the problem by requiring the first visitors to apply for tickets in advance and conducting them around the collections in small parties supervised by curators. These restrictions were lifted in 1810 and access gradually became easier until, by the end of the 19th century, the Museum opened seven days a week and on virtually all public holidays. Today around 5 million visitors come to Bloomsbury each year.

The Keeper of Antiquities wrote in 1851 that 'Europe cannot show any Building so ill adapted for its intended purpose, as the British Museum' but this to some extent reflected exasperation at the complexity of the building. The main Museum buildings consist of a neo-Classical core designed by Sir Robert Smirke and his brother Sydney, erected between the 1820s and 1850s. Sydney Smirke was responsible for the round Reading Room (1857). The latest addition is the Queen Elizabeth II Great Court, a Millennium Project designed by Lord Foster of Thames Bank, OM, which was opened in 2000.

An ever-present theme throughout the Museum's history has been shortage of money. Funded initially on the proceeds of a scandalously conducted public lottery, as capital diminished, government grants began to be made, and from 1801 regular annual funding was provided by Parliament. Whilst the Museum would not have developed without the generosity of private donors, Parliament financed the great 19th-century building programme and later projects, and also provided grants for the acquisition of objects. Some of the prices for which objects were acquired and buildings erected are cited here as evidence of continuing support from many sources.

Today the British Museum is one of the world's handful of large-scale universal museums, concerned not just with 'art' but with cultural history from prehistoric times to the present day. It has been likened to 'the world in a box', 'the memory of mankind', 'an enormous mind'. In 1778 John van Rymsdyk wrote 'It is Matchless! There is certainly no Mine, or Treasure like this in Europe . . . nor can such a one ever be compiled again unless by a Miracle'. How much more true is this statement today.

'Dr Mortimer, secretary to the Royal society, conducted their Royal Highnesses into the room where Sir Hans was sitting, being antient and infirm. The Prince took a chair and sat down by the good old gentleman some time, when he expressed the great esteem and value he had for him personally, and how much the learned world was obliged to him for his having collected such a vast library of curious books, and such immense treasures of the valuable and instructive productions of nature and art...

Their royal highnesses were not wanting in expressing their satisfaction and pleasure at seeing a collection, which surpass'd all the notions or ideas they had formed from even the most favourable accounts of it. The Prince... express'd the great pleasure it gave him to see so magnificent a collection in England, esteeming it an ornament to the nation; and expressed his sentiments how much it must conduce to the benefit of learning, and how great an honour will redound to Britain, to have it established for publick use to the latest posterity.'

Visit by the Prince and Princess of Wales to Sir Hans Sloane at his Manor House, Chelsea. Gentleman's Magazine, *1748*

1 Left: Sir Hans Sloane (1660–1753), founder of the British Museum. On his death his collection consisted of a miscellany of around 71,000 objects, 337 volumes of dried plants, and 50,000 printed books, prints, drawings and manuscripts. It was estimated to have cost Sloane £100,000.

2 Above: Sir Hans Sloane's memorial in Chelsea Old Churchyard, Cheyne Walk, where he was buried on 18 January 1753 'with great funeral pomp'. Parliament accepted Sloane's bequest of his collection and on 7 June 1753 the British Museum Act received the royal assent.

3 One of a selection of butterflies, largely 'milkweeds' (*Danainae*), preserved between sheets of mica, from the collection of the apothecary James Petiver (c. 1663–1718) which was bought by Sloane in 1718 for £4,000. (Natural History Museum)

4 Right: An Asante drum from Ghana, from the Sloane collection. Acquired in Virginia c. 1730. The wood is African and the drum may, therefore, have been brought from Africa on a slave ship. H. 40 cm

5 Right, top: Robert Harley, 1st Earl of Oxford (1661–1728), who laid the foundations of the Harleian library. The books were auctioned but around 7,660 volumes of manuscripts, plus 14,236 original rolls, charters, deeds and other legal documents were in 1753 bought by Parliament for the Museum for £10,000.

6 Left, bottom: Edward Harley, 2nd Earl of Oxford (1689–1741), began his collecting career with excessive book bills at college and went on to spend much of his wife's fortune of £500,000 in extending his father's collection.

7 Portrait of the early English poet Geoffrey Chaucer (c.1343–1400) from the manuscript of Thomas Hoccleve's early 15th-century *De regimine principum* in the Harleian collection. (British Library)

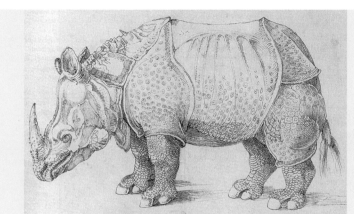

8 Left: Albrecht Dürer (1471–1528), *The Rhinoceros*, drawn in 1515 from reports, not from life. Sloane's collection included a large black leather-bound album which contained the majority of the Museum's present collection of 138 drawings attributed to Dürer. The album, acquired by Sloane in Holland in 1724, was marked '1637' and may have belonged at one time to Pieter Spiering Silfvercrona (d. 1652), a wealthy art collector from The Hague. *27.4 x 42 cm*

9 Right: Sloane's catalogue of his collection includes the 'Sloane astrolabe': 'A brasse astrolabe made at London for the latitudes of Rome, London etc. with a perpetuall almanack upon it'. It is probably the earliest surviving English astrolabe, made c.1295, and one of three he owned. *Diam. 46 cm*

10 Above: 'Carpet page' from St Mark's Gospel, Lindisfarne Gospels. Written and illuminated in honour of God and St Cuthbert c.AD 698, probably by the monk and Bishop Eadfrith, on Holy Island (Lindisfarne), Northumberland. The Cotton collection also included two of the four surviving copies of Magna Carta and the manuscript of the Anglo-Saxon poem *Beowulf*. (British Library)

11 Left: Lower Palaeolithic flint handaxe, about 350,000 years old, found in 1696 with the remains of a prehistoric elephant (thought to have been drowned in Noah's flood or imported by invading Romans in AD 43), the first recorded discovery of a prehistoric stone implement in Britain. Listed in Sloane's catalogue as 'A British *weapon* found wt Elephants tooth opposite to black Marys near Grayes inn lane. *Conyers*. It is a large black *flint* shaped into the figure of a Spears point.' The Museum now has about 2 million flints. *L. 16.5 cm*

12 Sir Robert Bruce Cotton (1571–1631), founder of a collection of 958 volumes of manuscripts given to the nation in 1700 by his descendants. The Museum in 1753 acquired 861 volumes and some fragments which had survived a fire in Ashburnham House in 1731. Cotton was able to acquire much material which had been dispersed following Henry VIII's dissolution of the monasteries.

'The British Museum, consisting of the immense collections of Sloane and the Royal Society [*sic*], will soon begin to be placed in Montague house, but the whole undertaking can hardly be accomplished in the space of ten years. When complete, this Museum will alone well repay the trouble of a visit to England. Both these collections however are at present in the greatest confusion, and many articles have been lost, either through neglect, or from being placed in a bad situation, but they receive acquisitions daily from every part of the globe.'
Letter from Dr Peter Ascanius to Carl Linnaeus, 1755

2 Inner coffin of Irtyru, 26th dynasty, *c.* 550 BC, from Memphis. The first mummy to enter the Museum's collections, it was bequeathed in 1756 by Colonel William Lethieullier who had visited Egypt in 1721. The collections were beginning to grow by gift although much that was offered would have been more at home in an earlier cabinet of curiosities.
L. 1.99 m

1 Montagu House, Bloomsbury, South Front and Courtyard, *c.* 1714. The house, designed by Robert Hooke, was built for Ralph, Duke of Montagu, in 1676. Damaged by fire in 1686, it was rebuilt and purchased by the Museum in 1754–5 for £10,000. The façade was probably original. The printed books were arranged on the ground floor, and manuscripts, natural history, antiquities and 'modern curiosities' on the first. The Museum opened to the public on 15 January 1759.

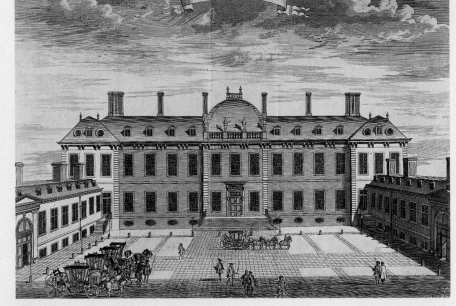

3 18th-century 'Instructions to Visitors'. Fearing unrestricted admission by the notoriously volatile London mob, the Trustees decided that visitors should be admitted by ticket only, applied for in advance, and conducted around the collections in small groups by the staff, the first of whom were appointed in 1756.

4 Right: Queen Mary's Psalter, English, early 14th century AD, from the Old Royal Library which King George II (1660–1727) presented to the Museum in 1757. With the library came the privilege of copyright deposit. The collection, now in the British Library, consisted of about 9,000 printed books and about 2,000 manuscripts. The psalter was given to Queen Mary Tudor by a customs officer who stopped it from being exported after the arrest of its owner, the Earl of Rutland, in 1553.

5 Painting of a dodo given to the Museum in 1759 and said to have been drawn from the living bird. Attributed to Roelandt Savery (1576–1639), it may have previously been in the Sloane collection. (Natural History Museum)

'On the 16th of November we went with our two travelling companions to see the British Museum, which deserves a full description. It originated in a bequest of Sir Hans Sloane, by whom the first foundation was laid; he was a rich man, who passed his life in collecting, at great expense, everything that seemed in any way remarkable. He is said to have spent about £50,000 upon the collection, the whole of which he left, when he died in 1753, for the benefit of the public, on condition that Parliament should pay his executors £20,000…

Everybody can obtain a ticket, and receive permission to enter the museum daily for some time to look over the books, and no servant or warder, etc., is allowed to receive a penny under penalty of dismissal. It is said that the wages of the people employed, and the cost of the maintenance of the building and objects, and the heating of the rooms, amount to £8000 annually.'
Count Frederick Kielmansegge, Diary of a Journey to England in the years 1761–2, *trans. Countess Kielmansegg*

1 Hellenistic Greek bronze head of a poet, 2nd century BC, perhaps the playwright Sophokles (c. 496–406 BC), given by the Earl of Exeter in 1760. Acquired in Constantinople in the early 17th century for the Earl of Arundel and later owned by the noted antiquary Dr Richard Mead (1673–1754). *H. 29.5 cm*

2 Above: The British Museum at Montagu House in Great Russell Street from the south-west. Preceding the Museum in this part of Bloomsbury were the 'Dog and Duck' (now the Museum Tavern) and St George's Church (consecrated in 1730).

THE
General Contents
OF THE
BRITISH MUSEUM:
WITH
REMARKS.
Serving as a
DIRECTORY
In Viewing that
Noble **CABINET**.

———

THE SECOND EDITION,
With ADDITIONS and IMPROVEMENTS, and a
COMPLETE INDEX.

———

Caſtor gaudet equis ; ovo prognatus eodem,
Pugnis : quot capitum vivunt, totidem ſtudiorum
Millia.

———

LONDON:
Printed for R. and J. DODSLEY, in *Pall-mall.*
MDCCLXII.
1762

3 Left: The first guidebook to the British Museum, written by Edmund Powlett 'to give a general Idea of the Contents of this wonderful Collection' (1761, 2nd edn 1762). It was soon apparent that the majority of visitors were easily bored with the outside of books and the occasional glimpse of a manuscript, and had mostly come to delight in the glittering natural history display, with its combination of science and sensation. Visitors were from 1761 permitted to agree democratically in which rooms they would spend the most time.

4 Left: One of a pair of 'very fine porcelain Jars of the Chelsea Manufactory, made in the year 1762, under the direction of Mr Sprimont, from a person unknown through Mr Empson' given in 1763. Known as the 'Cleopatra vases' since one shows the death of Cleopatra and the other the death of Harmonia (daughter of her and Mark Antony's patron deities), they were the first pieces of porcelain and the first 'modern' objects to be acquired. *H. 50 cm*

'April 3rd [1775]. Fair – I went to the British Museum – The sight was so various that it is hard to remember anything distinctly. – But what pleased me most was the ruins of Herculaneum. – The original magna charta of K John was in the Harleian (Cottonian) [*sic*] I think – The shell for which a cardinal gave 500£ I wd be sorry to give five pence for, unless merely because it is a specimen of human folly – The magnitude of the crocodile (20 feet) & the horn (5 feet at least) growing out of the nose of the unicorn fish were extraordinary – to me – The form of the pulpits was curious. A cylindrical form with spiral geometrical stairs issuing from the central upright. This evening I sketched out a letter on the method to read the Liturgy &c.

NB. The transparent picture of Vesuvius in the last eruption from the side, done by direction of Sir Wm Hamilton was very well.'
Dr Campbell's Diary of a Visit to England in 1775, *James C. Clifford (ed.) (1947)*

1 Sir Joshua Reynolds' portrait of Sir William Hamilton (1730–1803) – diplomat, volcanologist and antiquary – whose Classical collection, purchased in 1772 by a government grant of £8,410 plus £840 to house it, began the transformation of the Museum's collection of antiquities. The balance of the Museum began to change as the predominance of the library and natural history lessened. From its 18th-century beginnings, the Classical collection has developed into one of the most comprehensive in the world.

2 Above: 18th-century mourner's costume from Tahiti, probably that mentioned by Captain Cook in his journal in 1774, and given to the Museum by Cook in 1775 as part of 'A collection of artificial curiosities from the South Sea islands'. *H. 2.14m*

3 Red-figured water jar (*hydria*), signed by Meidias as potter and attributed to the 'Meidias painter', named from this vase. Made in Athens *c.* 425–400 BC, it is shown (bottom right) in Reynolds' portrait of Hamilton. Artists from the late 18th and 19th centuries often copied groups of figures from the vase as decoration. *H. 52.5 cm*

4 Right: The botanist Daniel Solander (1736–82) who joined the Museum in 1763 to catalogue the natural history collections, and in 1768 accompanied Banks on Cook's first voyage. He is depicted as a goose growing fat on Banks's patronage. The ethnographical and natural history collections were enriched by objects from Cook's voyages.

5 Portrait of Mary Davis of Great Saughall, near Cheshire, and her horns. The portrait was hung above the 'Cleopatra vases' (p. 9). Other curiosities included the 'Cyclops pig', the vegetable lamb of Tartary and a brick from the Tower of Babylon (*sic*).

6 Right: Plate (detail) from van Rymsdyk, illustrating a horn from the head of Mrs French of Tenterden, Kent, displayed in Montagu House in the room 'filled with Productions of Art, disposed in several Cabinets'.

7 Left: Jasperware portrait medallion of Captain James Cook (1728–79), explorer and circumnavigator, by Josiah Wedgwood, from a design by John Flaxman Jnr, c. 1784. A South Sea Room was opened in 1778 to house objects brought back from recent expeditions. The Museum's ethnographical collection is now the best in the world for range and quality. H. 10.6 cm

MUSEUM BRITANNICUM,
BEING AN
EXHIBITION
OF A GREAT VARIETY OF
ANTIQUITIES AND NATURAL CURIOSITIES,
BELONGING TO
THAT NOBLE AND MAGNIFICENT CABINET,
THE
BRITISH MUSEUM.
ILLUSTRATED WITH
CURIOUS PRINTS,
Engraved after the ORIGINAL DESIGNS, from NATURE, other OBJECTS;
AND WITH DISTINCT
EXPLANATIONS OF EACH FIGURE,
By JOHN and ANDREW VAN RYMSDYK, PICTORS.

When *Cicero* went to consult the *Oracle* about his future Conduct in Life, he received for Answer,

Follow Nature!

" No more you learned Fops, your Knowledge boast,
" Pretending all to know, by reading most,
" True Wit, by Inspiration, we obtain,
" Nature, not Art, Apollo's Wreath must gain.   Mrs. A. BEHN,
in Æsop's Life, 7th Plate.

LONDON:
Printed by I. MOORE, for the AUTHORS, CHARLES-STREET,
ST. JAMES'S-SQUARE. 1778.

8 Above: 18th-century Maori carved wooden treasure box (*wakahuia*) from New Zealand, collected on a Cook expedition. The Museum's collection is particularly rich in objects derived from first-time contact between Europeans and indigenous peoples. L. 59.5 cm

9 Left: Portrait (detail) of Sir Joseph Banks (1743–1820), botanist and plant collector, patron of Captain Cook's first (1768–71) voyage, and later, as President of the Royal Society, an influential *ex officio* Trustee of the Museum. In this portrait of 1771–2 Banks is wearing a Maori cloak brought back from Cook's voyages.

10 Above: Title page of *Museum Britannicum* by John and Andrew van Rymsdyk (1778), the first illustrated guide to the Museum, a somewhat idiosyncratic selection of objects such as an encrusted sword and skull from the Tiber, together with more conventional items like fossils, precious stones and birds' nests.

'I came to the Chevalier Hamilton's magnificent collection of Roman and Etrurian antiquities, which appears to contain some wonderful rarities. His life-size portrait hangs there too. This room alone rewards the student of history and of nature for his trip to England. Several Greek and Roman urns are to be seen; in one of the latter there is still a piece of asbestos in which the body was incinerated. These human ashes, whose lust for power sought to disturb peace and welfare all over the earth, are quite appropriately placed near some fragments of Vesuvius and Etna, which by means of forces supplied to them by nature, shattered the fatherland of these haughty conquerors, burying thousands of them beneath their glowing lava. With what sensations one handles a Carthaginian helmet excavated near Capua, household utensils from Herculaneum, ruined two thousand years ago, lachrymary vessels from the graves of Magna Graeca… Hamilton's room leads into that devoted to Captain Cook, that luckless, excellent man, and all the pots, weapons and clothes from the South Sea islands just recently discovered, are on view there, just as they are shown in the prints illustrating the description of his voyage: crowns, helmets and war-masks, state uniforms and mourning – the former made of tiny shells and feathers, very densely and neatly sewn on in strips according to colour, the latter also partly of feathers and partly of bast, and made out of linen from the so-called lace-bark tree.'

Sophie v. la Roche, Sophie in London *(1786), trans. Clare Williams (1936)*

1 The Grand Staircase of Montagu House with ceiling frescoes by Charles de Lafosse (1636–1716) depicting the fall of Phaeton, painted *c.* 1686. These disappeared, probably destroyed, when Montagu House was demolished in the 1840s. Watercolour by George Scharf Snr (1788–1860), in 1845, purchased from his widow 1862. The introduction of an admission charge in 1784 was shelved because visitors 'consisted chiefly of Mechanics and persons of the lower Classes' who would be unlikely to pay. *36.2 x 2.8 cm*

2 Above: Detail of Lafosse's drawing for the Montagu House ceiling: 'Diana, Aurora and the Morning Star with two Horae pouring Dew, by the Zodiacal Arc'. Presented by Miss Diane Nixon in 1998 through the American Friends of the British Museum. *22.6 x 32.4 cm*

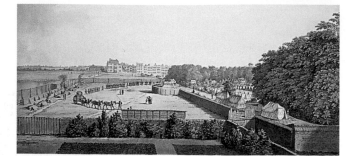

4 The Gordon Riots of 1780: Colonel Stanhope Harvey's York Regiment of Militia – around 700 soldiers with wives and children having arrived by forced march – parade in the gardens of Montagu House. In the distance can be seen the beginnings of Southampton Row. *36.4 x 53 cm*

3 Below: The blue jasperware 'Pegasus vase' given to the Museum in 1786 by the potter Josiah Wedgwood who was influenced by the Museum's collections and made drawings of vases there in 1769. Wedgwood described the vase as 'the finest & most perfect I have ever made'. The scene of the 'Apotheosis of Homer' was adapted by John Flaxman Jnr from a Greek vase in the Hamilton collection. *H. 46.4 cm*

'This museum is composed of manuscript and printed books; of Egyptian, Etruscan, Greek and Roman antiquities; Indian, Chinese, and Japanese idols; of the vestments, weapons, and utensils of the islanders of the South Seas and other savage nations; of quadrupeds, amphibious animals, birds, insects, fishes, shells, and other marine productions; of minerals, petrifactions, and fossils of every kind.

This immense assemblage of objects was partly formed by the celebrated Hans Sloane. It is a pity that the collection was not allowed to remain as he originally left it. Had no additions been made to it, and had it been allowed to retain the modest title of *Sloane's Museum*, many would doubtless have been anxious to visit the collection of that indefatigable naturalist, and would have viewed with as much astonishment as satisfaction, what the love of science, aided by an affluent fortune and liberal disposition, had been able to perform…

The British Museum contains many valuable collections in natural history; but, with the exception of some fishes in a small apartment, which are begun to be classed, nothing is in order, everything is out of its place; and this assemblage appears rather an immense magazine, in which things have been thrown at random, than a scientific collection, destined to instruct and honour a great nation.'
Barthelmi Faujas Saint-Fond, Travels in England, Scotland and the Hebrides *(1799)*

1 An Indian elephant by Rembrandt van Rijn (1606–69), one of four drawings probably made in 1637, and a treasure of the Cracherode collection. The great series of Rembrandt etchings was one of the strengths of Cracherode's print collection. Building on gifts such as this, today the Department of Prints & Drawings has one of the world's greatest collections, consisting of approx. 2½ million prints and 60,000 drawings. *17.9 x 25.6 cm*

2 Left: The only likeness of the reclusive connoisseur the Revd Clayton Mordaunt Cracherode (1730–99) who used his fortune of around £31,000 a year to purchase 'fewer and better rather than more and worse'. His bequest of 4,500 rare books, 662 drawings, 5–10,000 prints (the exact number is not known because of a theft which occurred not long after their acquisition), coins, gems and a small cabinet of minerals greatly enriched the Museum's collections.

3 Among the coins in the fine cabinet bequeathed by Cracherode was this tetradrachm from Naxos, Greek Sicily, *c.* 460 BC, depicting the satyr Silenus, with animal's ears and a bushy tail, holding a wine-cup. The coins of Sicily are some of the most beautiful ever made. *Diam. 26 mm*

4 Right: Admission ticket for a tour of the Museum in 1790. Admission was free but the Trustees waged a continuous battle to prevent the staff soliciting tips from visitors.

This Ticket entitles _____ to a Sight of the **BRITISH MUSEUM,** at the Hour of One on Wednesday the 3 of March 1790. No Money is to be given to the Servants.

5 Right: Montagu House with its 'ever smoking chimneys' seen from the north-east, *c.* 1800. The appointment in 1799 of the energetic Joseph Planta (1744–1827) as Principal Librarian was the prelude to many changes and a greater professionalism.

'The British Museum is situated on the North side of Great Russel-street Bloomsbury. The site is a square, inclosed by a high blank brick wall, which excludes the house from view in every direction on that side. At each corner is a turret, and over the great Ionic arch of entrance a large and handsome cupola. Upon entering the court, the spectator finds himself in a grand Colonade of Ionic pillars, extremely chaste and well proportioned, which extends the whole length of the front. At the East and West ends of the quadrangle are the lodgings of the different officers, connecting the Colonade and Museum... On the West side of the house is a flower-garden and a terrace, disposed with much taste, and shaded by numbers of flourishing trees and shrubs... The basement story contains the largest and most repelling specimens of Nature and Art.

The ponderous spoils of our Egyptian campaign are at present under two temporary sheds in the quadrangle. Of those the huge baths and coffins covered with hieroglyphicks are the most interesting. To which may be added the deities, the enormous clenched hand, and excellent ram's head, in friable stone, together with coffins, fragments of grand columns, and two Romans in statuary marble.'
James Peller Malcolm, Londinium Redivivum... (1803)

1 The Staircase of Montagu House in 1808. In that year the first official Synopsis (guide to the Museum) was published, and the Department of Prints & Drawings opened its first students' room. However it was not until 1810 that 'persons of decent appearance' were allowed to wander unescorted on certain days.

2 Above: The Rosetta Stone, key to the decipherment of ancient Egyptian hieroglyphs, bearing a decree written in three scripts, issued on 27 March 196 BC at Memphis, in honour of Ptolemy V Epiphanes. It was found by a French engineer at el-Rashid (Rosetta) in 1799, ceded with other antiquities to the British Crown in 1801 under the Treaty of Alexandria, and given by George III in 1802. H. 1.14 m (max.)

3 Below: Townley's favourite sculpture, 'Clytie' – a marble funerary portrait, probably of a wealthy woman, c. AD 40–50, copying the style of Antonia (d. AD 38), daughter of Mark Antony and Octavia. Purchased by Townley from Prince Laurenzano of Naples in 1772, the figure enjoyed huge popularity and influenced English artists and craftsmen. H. 57 cm

4 Left: Exterior of the Townley Gallery, designed by George Saunders (c. 1762–1839) and opened in 1808, showing (left) the connection with Montagu House. This was the first purpose-built exhibition gallery. A Committee had been formed in 1802 to consider expanding the Museum's buildings. 18.3 x 24.9 cm

6 Right: Napoleon invaded Egypt in 1798, taking with him more than 150 scholars and artists to record its marvels. Here, members of the expedition inspect a fist from a colossal red granite statue of Ramesses II, c. 1250 BC. Said to be from the temple of Ptah, Memphis, the fist was among the antiquities ceded by the French and given to the Museum by George III in 1802. *L. (of fist) 1.3 m (max.)*

5 Below: Charles Townley (1737–1805) and an ideal depiction of his collection in his library at his home in Park Street, Westminster (1781). The objects were purchased from collectors and dealers in Rome largely between 1768 and 1774 – Discobolus was painted in later. Townley bequeathed the collection to his family, directing that they establish a new museum. Unable to do so, they sold it to the Government for £20,000 and a place on the Museum's Board of Trustees. It is a rare example of an intact 18th-century collection. Townley's archive was bought in 1995 with the aid of the NHMF, BMF and Caryatids. *12.7 x 9.9 cm*

7 Right: 'Discobolus' (the discus-thrower) from the Townley collection, one of several Roman copies after a lost Greek bronze original by the sculptor Myron, 5th century BC. Found in the villa of the Emperor Hadrian at Tivoli in 1791 and bought by Townley in 1793. The head was restored, wrongly, in the 18th century. *H. 1.7 m*

8 Sarcophagus of Nectanebo II, last native pharaoh of Egypt (r. 360–343 BC), c. 343 BC, given by George III in 1802. It was found in the Attarin Mosque at Alexandria, having been used as a ritual bath. At first thought to have been the sarcophagus of Alexander the Great, this was disproved once the hieroglyphs could be translated. *L. (of sarcophagus) 3.14 m*

'There is now light and length of day sufficient to see the sights of this capital. We have begun by the British Museum. The building is disposed round a vast court, and in very good taste. You have to wait in the hall of entrance till fourteen other visitors are assembled, for the rule is, that fifteen persons are to be admitted at one time, neither more nor less. This number completed, a German cicerone took charge of us, and led us *au pas de charge* through a number of rooms full of stuffed birds and animals; – many of them seemingly in a state of decay. We had a glimpse of arms, dresses, and ornaments of savages hung around; – of a collection of minerals; – next of antiquities from Herculaneum and Pompeia and monstrous Egypt. We remarked a treble inscription on a large block of dark porphyry, brought from Rosetta; one in hieroglyphics, one in the common language of Egypt, and one in Greek; – all three saying the same thing serve as a glossary to each other… The last and most valuable acquisitions are the Greek and Roman marbles brought from Italy by Mr Townley. The merit, however, of a considerable part of these marbles consists mostly of their being undoubtedly antique.'

Louis Simond, Journal of a Tour and Residence in Great Britain, during the years 1810 and 1811, by a French traveller *(1817)*

1 'Mortality weighs heavily on me like unwilling sleep' wrote the poet Keats on first seeing the sculptures of the Parthenon, and in his 'Ode on a Grecian urn' (1819) he described a sacrificial victim: a 'heifer lowing at the skies', portrayed in the Parthenon frieze. H. 1 m (approx.)

3 Below: The horse of Selene, the Moon goddess, from the east pediment of the Parthenon, one of a series of drawings made by the artist Benjamin Haydon (1786–1846) in 1809 when the sculptures were at Lord Elgin's house in Park Lane prior to their acquisition by the Museum. From an album of 264 drawings purchased from F.W. Haydon in 1881 for £75, the price having been reduced because the Museum was short of funds. 55.4 x 75.9 cm

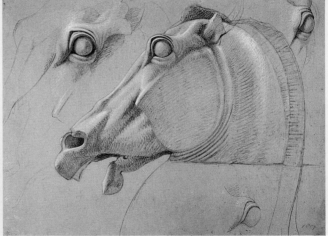

2 The Museum's Trustees in the 'Temporary Elgin Room', designed by Sir Robert Smirke and erected in 1817 to house the Parthenon sculptures. The collection, which included other material such as a colossal scarab from Constantinople, was bought from Lord Elgin by the British government for £35,000 and, by Act of Parliament, transferred to the British Museum.

4 Left: 'Polar treasures' from John Ross's expedition to Baffin Bay are brought to the Museum in 1818. Curators dancing on the parapet of Montagu House can be glimpsed in the background.

6 Reception attended by over 30,000 people at Kumasi, modern Ghana, for the 1817 expedition by the African Company to improve Asante–British relations. From T.E. Bowdich's *Mission from Cape Coast Castle to Ashantee* (1819), 'one of the most vivid and detailed accounts of an African kingdom ever written'.

5 Bust of Ramesses II (known as the 'Younger Memnon'), *c.* 1250 BC, acquired in 1816 by Belzoni from the King's mortuary temple at Thebes, and given by the British Consul-General in Cairo, Henry Salt (1780–1827), and the explorer Jean-Louis Burckhardt (1784–1817). The head, which arrived in 1818, was perhaps the first piece of Egyptian sculpture to be recognised as a work of art by connoisseurs who had traditionally made judgements by the standards of ancient Greek art. *H. 2.67 m*

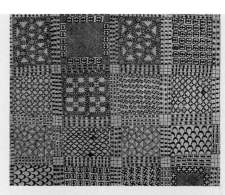

7 'A Mourning cloth, wove in Dagwumba, but painted in Ashantee', part of a collection of around thirty objects from Ghana given to the Museum by T.E. Bowdich (1791–1824) in 1818, one of the earliest attempts by a European to make a systematic collection from an African society.

8 Above: Brass anti-slavery medal, London, *c.* 1787, from the collection made by Sarah Sophia Banks (1744–1818) and acquired after her death. Among her coins were some of the earliest issues from the new United States of America. Miss Banks also bequeathed a pioneering collection of ephemera: some 20,000 items including trade cards, invitations, lottery tickets, turnpike tickets and election cards. *Diam. 34 mm*

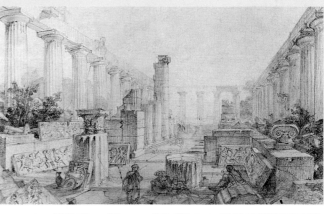

9 Right: Portrait of the Italian Giovanni-Battista Belzoni (1778–1823) – circus strongman, hydraulic engineer and explorer – who was responsible for the excavation of a number of Egyptian tombs and temples.

10 Right, top: The Temple of Apollo Epikourios at Bassae in Phigaleia, Greece, 420–400 BC, after excavation. The site was first noted by Western travellers in 1765, but it was not until 1811 that a group of artists and architects discovered the sculptures which were bought at auction by the British government for £15,000.

11 Above: Herakles and the Amazon Queen Hippolyte from the Bassae frieze (the Phigaleian marbles) which reached the Museum in 1815. Drawing from a 19th-century guidebook. *H. (of sculptures) 64 cm*

'ANTE-ROOM. This room contains one object of very great value and interest. It was long known as the Barberini Vase, from the name of the family in whose palace it was for several generations deposited. It has latterly been called the Portland Vase; – having been purchased off Sir William Hamilton by the Duchess of Portland, and afterwards presented [*sic*] to the Museum by the Duke of Portland. This vase is only a few inches high, and is formed of a dark blue glass, on the surface of which a white incrustation has been deposited, and then the outer material sculpted down, so as to leave the white figures in relief on the dark ground, in the manner of cameos cut on onyx. The whole object offers a beautiful specimen of Greek art; but the design and sculpture are not so admirable as the high reputation which this vase has always enjoyed would lead us to expect. The subject of the design has never yet been satisfactorily explained; but it is, no doubt, connected with some sepulchral rites; as the vase was found at a short distance from Rome, about the middle of the 16th century, in a sepulchral chamber, and was inclosed in a marble sarcophagus. The room also contains one or two curious specimens of ancient Fresco Painting.'

A Guide to the Beauties of the British Museum, being a critical and descriptive account of the principal works of art contained in the gallery of antiquities of the above national collection (1826)

1 Left: Bronze head of an athlete, southern Etruscan, *c*. 300–250 BC. From the bequest by a Museum Trustee Richard Payne Knight (1751–1824) which comprised 5,000 coins, 111 gems, 1,144 drawings, 800 bronzes, as well as sculptures and other material. Said by Knight to have been the first item to enter his collection. *H. 21.5 cm*

2 Above: Federico Barocci (1535–1612), *Landscape with Bank and Trees*, *c*. 1590. From the Payne Knight bequest of drawings, 'undoubtedly one of the major collections of this type formed in this country'. *39.3 x 24.9 cm*

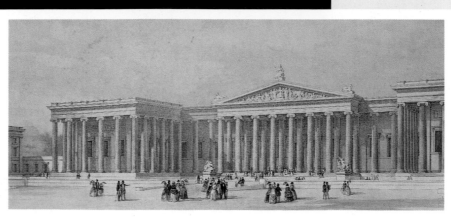

3 Right: Artist's impression of the South Front showing sculptural decoration, intended but not executed. Although Sir Robert Smirke's plans were first approved in 1823, the general plan was not published until 1836 and the front elevation in 1843. *40.7 x 58.1 cm*

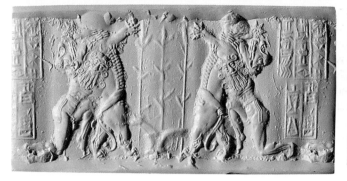

4 Left: Akkadian period cylinder seal, c. 2250 BC, from the collection made by Claudius James Rich (1787–1821), the East India Company's Resident in Baghdad. The beginnings of the Ancient Near Eastern collections are to be discerned in the purchase from his widow in 1825 of 800 manuscripts (£5,500), coins (£1,000) and 'Babylonish and Nineveh gems and antiquities' (£1,000). H. 3.6 cm

5 Left, below: Gilded lacquer and wood Buddha from Rangoon, Burma, late 18th to early 19th century, given by Captain Frederick Marryat RN in 1826. An attempt to make the gift dependent on Marryat's being appointed a hereditary Museum Trustee was refused. H. (excl. modern base) 1.48 m

6 Left: In 1823 King George IV gave his father's library (the King's Library) to the nation, and parliament allocated £40,000 to house it in the British Museum. This provided the catalyst for the architect Sir Robert Smirke (1780–1867) to begin his quadrangular neo-classical building. The East Wing, built to store the King's Library, was completed in 1827. Watercolour, c. 1850, by Eugene Armand Roy. Given by a descendant of the artist in 2003. 29 x 21 cm

7 Left: 6th- to 5th-century BC relief from the Apadana (audience hall) at the Persian royal capital of Persepolis, showing guardsmen in Persian dress. 'Tolerably fair specimens' collected by Sir Gore Ouseley (1770–1844) during his 'Embassy to the Court of Persia' (1811–14) and given to the Museum in 1825. H. 60 cm

8 Left: Sketch by George Scharf Snr of visitors to the Museum in 1828. The Museum recorded 127,643 visitors in 1825. It was now receiving annual grants from Parliament (£12,877 in 1827).

'23 October 1833. Took a stroll over the British Museum, which I had not seen since the new buildings – Went up the old Staircase with painted walls & ceiling, with the 2 old Stuffed Cameleopards going to decay, into the room containing feathered idols of hideous aspect & clubs, weapons, utensils & canoes of various Savage nations looking just as they used to do when I, a tiny urchin of 8 years of age, first saw them, proud of being arrived at such years of discretion, as gave me the privilege of entrée which I had often before sighed after, & of having my name enrolled in the venerable book, as a visitor – The next room was filled with cases of stuffed animals – Passing thro 2 rooms to the right containing Insects & Reptiles I entered the new part which is very handsome tho quite in a different style from the old…

There is a long suite of rooms the first 2 containing Birds arranged in very handsome glass cases around the walls, & with Table Cases with eggs, in the middle, & the 3rd & longest glazed Cases in rows – On a table made of various marbles there was a Tortoise beautifully carved out of a green stone called Nephrite & found at Allahabad in India.' Diary of Mr W.E. Maxwell

1 The Arched Room, added to the North Wing in 1837–9. Initially used for the storage of rare books, it has, since the departure of the British Library in the 1990s, been adapted as the students' room of the Department of the Ancient Near East, holding their library, archive and collection of cuneiform tablets. It is the last virtually untouched library room in this area; the others were in the 1930s filled with mezzanine floors for book storage and offices.

2 Below: A king clutching a sword, from 'A set of very curious and ancient chessmen' made of walrus ivory and whales' teeth, found on the Isle of Lewis, Outer Hebrides, probably made in Norway c. AD 1150–1200. Sixty-seven chess pieces, fourteen counters and a belt buckle were purchased in 1831 from an Edinburgh dealer for 80 guineas. In 1888 a further eleven were bought by the National Museum of Scotland. H. 10.2 cm (max.)

3 Above: The celebrated 'Tablet of Abydos', a list of Egyptian Kings, c. 1270 BC, from the Temple of Ramesses II at Abydos, discovered in 1819 by W.J. Bankes (1786–1855). Purchased for £560 at the 1837 Paris sale of the collection of Jean François Mimaut (1774–1837), Consul-General of France in Egypt in 1829. Mimaut's son-in-law and the Trustees considered that, as 'the most valuable document in existence for assisting in fixing the chronological series of Egyptian Kings' it should join the Rosetta Stone at the Museum. H. (of detail) 1.35 m

4 Above: Gilded bronze statue of the Buddhist goddess Tara from Sri Lanka. Given in 1830 by Sir Robert Brownrigg (1759–1833), first Governor of Ceylon. H. 1.43 m

5 Below: Jade terrapin, 17th century AD: 'While the General [Alexander Kyd] was employed, a number of years ago, as Engineer in the East India Company's Service, about the Fortifications at Allahabad, some work people brought to him the said Tortoise which had been found at the bottom of a Tank' (pond). Kyd (1754–1826) intended that it should eventually come to the Museum but it was not donated until 1830 by Thomas Wilkinson. *L. 48.5 cm*

6 Above: The Etruscan Room (now Room 72), in Smirke's Upper West Wing, the northern section of which opened in 1837.

7 Right: Ku-ka'ili-moku, the 'island snatcher', a Hawaiian war god from one of the temples erected by King Kamehameha I, unifier of the Hawaiian islands. Probably made AD 1790–1810. Described in the acquisitions register as 'A large wooden idol from Otaheite presented by Mr W. Howard' (1839). *H. 2.72 m*

8 Above: Colossal red granite head found in the temple of Khonspekhrod in the precincts of the Temple of Mut, Thebes, c. 1350 BC, possibly Amenhotep III. Henry Salt (1780–1827) was British Consul-General in Egypt 1816–27. He employed men such as Belzoni to excavate at sites including Thebes, Giza and Abu Simbel. The Museum failed to take full advantage of his collecting activity and many objects went elsewhere. However, some antiquities were purchased at the sale of his collection by Sotheby's in 1835. *H. 2.87 m*

9 Above: Athenian amphora (wine-jar) made by the potter Exekias, showing Achilles killing the Amazon Queen Penthesilea, Athens, c. 540–530 BC, found at Vulci, Italy. Bought at the sale of the collections of the Chevalier Durand in 1836. The Museum acquired the major part of Durand's collection of Greek vases for about £3,000 having consulted the Danish antiquary P.O. Brønsted. The Museum was now beginning to profit from the dispersal of some of the great continental collections but still had to collect within Treasury constraints. *H. 41.6 cm*

10 Left: Prehistoric gold cape, c. 1900–1600 BC. Found at Mold, Wales, in 1833 around the bones of a skeleton in a burial chamber by workmen quarrying for stone in an ancient burial mound named Bryn yr Ellyllon (the Fairies' or Goblins' Hill). Purchased for £95 in 1836, additional fragments were later given to the Museum. *H. 23.5 cm*

'27 March 1841. At a quarter after Three today Her Majesty and His Royal Highness Prince Albert visited the Museum... They left at 5.25... The two Senior Officers, where there were two, were named to Her Majesty at the entrance of each Department, in the same manner as was done in 1808 to Queen Charlotte... In the King's Library the richer specimens of that collection only were laid out... In the Egyptian Room the head of Memnon, the Rosetta Inscription, the Paintings and Lord Prudhoe's lions were the great attraction... The Ladies of the Officers families were assembled in the great central saloon... The Elgin Room was an attraction for a considerable time... In the Medal Room, the Syracusan Coins in silver and the Gold ornaments were laid out in one part, and a rich series of Gold Medals mostly from George the Third's Cabinet on the other. On leaving this Room Prince Albert told me Her Majesty was not desirous to see the Egyptian mummies. We however went through the Room saw the old wig from Thebes and then into the Etruscan Room, when Her Majesty admired the forms especially of many of the Vases. The Mineral Gallery was next visited, where the Saurian Fossils are exhibited in the Wall cases... In the Print Room Her Majesty had placed before her... the Cellini Cup, a selection from the finest Drawings of Rembrandt, Claude Lorraine, Leonardo da Vinci, and Rubens.'

Diaries of Sir Henry Ellis, Principal Librarian of the British Museum (1827–56). *British Library, Additional MS 36,653*

1 Entrance to Montagu House. Demolition of Montagu House began in 1842 but the gatehouse remained until 1850. The military guard was introduced in 1807 and stayed until 1863, when it was replaced by the Metropolitan Police.

2 Relief panel from the 'Harpy Tomb', Xanthos, a pillar of grey-blue limestone 2.1 metres square, standing on a tall plinth, erected c. 480–460 BC. H. (of relief) 1.02 m

3 Right: Bronze model of a horse's head, c. AD 40–80. Part of a hoard of about 140 objects, including many items of horse harness, buried AD 50–100 and found at Stanwick, Yorkshire, in 1844. Their gift to the Museum in 1847 by Lord Prudhoe (later Duke of Northumberland) was made dependent on the provision of a room for the display of British antiquities, which opened in 1852. Some of the pressure to exhibit British material arose because of the increasing amount now being uncovered, particularly by railway excavations. L. 10 cm

4 Left: Drawing by George Scharf Jnr (1820–95) in 1840 or 1842 of the Harpy Tomb at Xanthos, ancient capital of Lykia (Asia Minor). The tomb was excavated by Sir Charles Fellows (1799–1860) who first visited the area in 1838. In the 1840s he acquired for the Museum remains of a number of tombs, among them the Nereid and Payava monuments, the Harpy Tomb and the Lion Tomb.

5 The nabob of Surat and his entourage in the Mineral Gallery in 1844. Watercolour by George Scharf Snr, one of his studies of foreigners in London. *14.1 x 23.4cm*

6 Stone seated figure of the Aztec fire god Xiuhtecuhtli, *c.* 1325–1521, from a collection of antiquities taken to Spain after Mexico's independence in 1821, and later acquired by John Wetherell. In 1849, when the collection was bought for £200, he wrote of his 'Mexicans', 'it wd flatter me to see them merit a place in that distinguish'd establishment' [the Museum]. *H. 32cm*

7 Right: 'The British Museum 2043, Curiosities of Ancient Times'. A group of future visitors to the Museum inspect political specimens – a Whig and a Tory. Drawing by George Cruikshank (1792–1878) made in 1842 for the *Comic Almanack*. 4,260 etchings, 4,065 drawings by Cruikshank and 2,637 prints by other artists were bequeathed by his widow in 1884. *22.7 x 18.7 cm (page)*

8 Left: 10th-century AD hoard of Viking silver and coins, the largest yet found in north-west Europe, discovered at Cuerdale on the banks of the River Ribble in Lancashire in 1840, and probably buried *c.* AD 905. Found in 'a leaden chest which, except for a few fragments, had corroded and fallen to pieces'. When spread out it covered an entire room and consisted of around 7,500 coins and 1,100 items of silver bullion (approx. 40 kg). Queen Victoria, who owned the hoard as Duke of Lancaster, in 1841 gave the Museum 1,440 coins and 744 pieces of silver.

9 Right: Watercolour of the decorative design for the Front Hall by L.W. Collmann (1847). The figures are said to be by Alfred Stevens (1818–75). The Hall, opened on 19 April 1847, completed Robert Smirke's quadrangle. (He had retired in 1846 and been succeeded by his brother Sydney.) The decoration survived until the bombing of the Second World War. It was recreated in 2000. *51.2 x 68.4cm*

10 Drawing of the 'Black Obelisk of Shalmaneser III' (r. 858–824 BC), from Nimrud, erected *c.* 825 BC. It was found by A.H. Layard in 1846 'lying on its side, ten feet below the surface', and acquired in 1848. In the second register Jehu, King of Israel, pays tribute to the Assyrian King. The decipherment of cuneiform was greatly helped by this well-preserved text. Layard first visited Assyrian sites in 1840 and returned in 1845 to excavate, with Museum funding from 1846. He left archaeology to become an MP in 1851. *H. (of obelisk) 1.98 m*

'BRITISH MUSEUM – THE CHRISTMAS HOLIDAYS. On Monday last the scene presented at this public institution was of the most gratifying description. At the hour of opening, streams of school boys and girls, and family groups, both town and country bred, might be seen flowing along the streets towards the main entrance… The bulk of the visitors evidently belonged to the working classes, and it was pleasant to see the comfortable and well-clad appearance of the majority. The conduct of all was admirable, and although in the course of Monday upwards of forty-two thousand persons were admitted, no case of intoxication or ill-behaviour was noticed. Such a gathering as this was creditable to the intelligent part of the working population of the metropolis; and although it must be admitted that some passed by the rare objects collected here in a somewhat hurried manner, having scarcely learnt to see; it is certain that not even the most careless can pass through these galleries without gathering wholesome materials for future thoughts.'
The Builder, *1 January 1859*

1 With the completion of the forecourt in 1852, the first stage of the Smirke plan had been achieved. However, the round Reading Room had to be erected 1854–7 in the central courtyard to cope with the increasing flood of books. An informal opening by Prince Albert had been arranged for 2 May 1857, but due to a death in the royal family the Prince was unable to come and the proceedings were over by 3 pm. By 1860 the library had expanded to around 600,000 printed books, much faster than its continental competitors. Its successor, today's British Library, has 16 million books and periodical volumes.

2 Karl Marx (1818–83), who obtained his first reader's ticket in 1850. When applying for a ticket in 1879, his daughter Eleanor wrote: 'My father, Dr Karl Marx, visited the Reading Room daily for nearly 30 years.' As Mikhail Gorbachev remarked during a visit in 1984, some of the complaints about communism could be directed to the British Museum.

3 Below: The Lothar crystal, probably made AD 855–869. Purchased for £267 in 1855 at the Christie's sale of the collection of Ralph Bernal (c. 1783–1854) at which the Museum, working with the V&A, made a number of spectacular acquisitions. The crystal was in the abbey of Waulsort in Belgium from the 10th century until 1793 when the monks were dispersed in the French Revolution. It was said to have been offered for sale by a Belgian dealer in the mid-19th century with a story that it had been fished up out of the River Meuse. If so, the crack might have occurred when it was thrown into the river. According to the Museum's records, the crystal was bought by a Mr Pratt from a Belgian dealer for 12 francs and sold to Bernal for £10. *Diam. 11.5 cm*

4 The 'Battersea shield' – a Celtic shield of bronze and enamel, c. 2nd or 1st century BC, found in the bed of the River Thames near Battersea, probably deposited there as a ritual sacrifice. Following the appointment of A.W. Franks (p. 29) in 1851, the Museum began methodically to collect British material such as this. Purchased in 1857 for £40. *L. 77.7 cm*

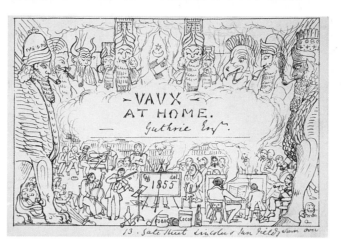

5 W.S.W. Vaux's (Keeper of Coins and Medals, 1861–70) 'At Home' card inspired by the Assyrian gateway figures. From the 18th century, senior staff and their families lived in residences on site. Vaux moved in on his appointment to the Keepership.

6 Left: Photograph of the South Front, c. 1857, by Roger Fenton (1819–69), better known for his photographs of the Crimean War. Fenton was employed by the Museum in 1853 and used a 'photographic house' on the roof. He left a collection of 250 photographs of Classical sculpture, Old Master drawings, cuneiform tablets and views of the building prior to his leaving the Trustees' service in an economy drive.

7 Above: A.H. Layard's excavations in Assyria (modern Iraq). Watercolour probably made by the expedition's professional artist Frederick Cooper, c. 1850.

8 Right: Sir Charles Newton with the lion of Knidos, late 4th to early 3rd century BC, found in 1858 on a promontory overlooking the sea by his architectural draughtsman, Richard Pullan. A zig-zag roadway was constructed on the mountainside down which the lion and its case, weighing 11 tons, were hauled for three days by 300 men before being lowered onto a raft and then transferred to a Royal Navy ship. L. (of lion) 3 m

9 Right: 'Saron' (instrument with metal keys) from the set of Indonesian musical instruments (gamelan) acquired in the early 19th century by Sir Stamford Raffles (1781–1826), and given to the Museum in 1859, with other items, by his nephew after an unsuccessful attempt at sale. Raffles, a keen linguist and zoologist, was appointed Lieutenant Governor of Java in 1811. During his time there he amassed an important collection which included musical instruments and puppets. L. 1 m

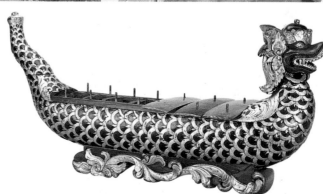

10 Above: Marble statue of the goddess Demeter, c. 350 BC, found in the sanctuary at Knidos (in modern Turkey) by Sir Charles Newton in 1858. The head was at first missing. Newton was Keeper of Greek & Roman Antiquities 1861–86. H. 1.47 m

11 Left: After Layard's departure Henry Creswicke Rawlinson, the East India Company's Resident in Baghdad, took over the general direction of excavations, continued from 1852 to 1854 by Hormuzd Rassam (1826–1910). At Nineveh Rassam discovered the relief sculptures of the lion hunt of Ashurbanipal, c. 645 BC, 'probably the finest animal scenes of antiquity'. *H. 16.5 cm*

14 Italian maiolica dish by Nicola da Urbino, c. 1525, with the arms, personal device and motto of Isabella d'Este. Acquired in 1855 at the sale of the collection of Ralph Bernal, described as 'one of the most discriminating collectors of all time'. Bernal's collection had cost him £20,000 but the sale lasted thirty-two days and realised three or four times what he had paid for it, an indication of rising prices in the art market. Shortly before the sale, as a device to induce the Trustees to take positive action, A.W. Franks (p. 29) presented some of his own maiolica. *Diam. 26.9 cm*

12 Above: Assyrian gateway figure from Layard's excavations at Nimrud being manoeuvred up the front steps on its arrival in 1852. In addition to sculptures, ivories and other objects, Layard's workmen, and subsequently his assistant Rassam, unearthed Ashurbanipal's library of cuneiform tablets, the study and decipherment of which formed the cornerstone of Assyriology.

13 Below: Sculpture from the Mausoleum at Halikarnassos (modern Bodrum, Turkey), erected c. 350 BC by Mausolos, ruler of Karia in south-west Asia Minor, and his wife Artemisia. The sculpture probably represents an ancestor of the ruling dynasty. Charles Newton (1816–94), then Vice consul at Mytilene and later Keeper of Greek & Roman Antiquities (1861–85), first visited Bodrum in 1852 and recognised a lion from the Mausoleum built into the castle wall. He began to dig in 1857, discovering fragments of the long-lost building. *H. 2.67 m*

15 In 1851 A.W. Franks (p. 29) joined the Museum to curate the British collections. An early success was the acquisition for £2,000 of Charles Roach Smith's (1807–90) collection (seen here) of around 5,000 objects – the first major collection of British archaeology to be purchased. Ranging from the 3rd millennium BC to the post-medieval, it was particularly rich in Romano-British and medieval objects, largely accumulated over twenty years in London. It also included important Anglo-Saxon coins, brooches and axe- and spear-heads, particularly from the River Thames, and some comparative material from England and the Continent.

'March 27 [1863], Friday. To-day we all went to see the British Museum. Aunt Bunsen knows Professor Owen, a man who gives his whole life to studying antiquities particularly fossils and skeletons, & so she asked him to let us all go with him to see some of the things there, & he said he would explain it. We went to see the great bones and he explained a great many of them, but he spoke in such a low voice that some could not hear, the principal thing that we had come to see was a most remarkable fossil bird which had been found imbedded in stone, & only discovered last year, but it lived such a long time ago, that when it was alive none of the chalk was made, and as all the chalk is made of old animals ground to powder who lived long before the Deluge, it must have lived millions of years ago.

But it was most remarkably perfect and we could see each feather and each bone, but the head was gone, probably it had been eaten by some wild beast...

Louisa is going to school on Easter Tuesday at Miss Clarence's near Brighton where there are 27 girls.'
Ellen Buxton's Journal, 1860–1864, E.R.C. Creighton (ed.) (1967)

1 Statue from Easter Island (Chile), known as Hoa Hakananai'a ('Stolen' or 'Hidden' Friend), *c.* AD 1000, brought back by the crew of HMS Topaze following a visit to Easter Island in 1868 on a surveying expedition. Given to the Museum in 1869 by Queen Victoria. The statue was found partly buried inside a stone house at the ritual centre of Orongo and bore traces of red and white colouring. This colouring was lost during the transfer of the 4-ton statue to the ship by raft. *H. 2.42 m*

STATUE OF
HOA-HAKA-NANA-IA.
EASTER ISLAND.
PRESENTED BY H.M. THE QUEEN, 1869.
BROUGHT HOME BY H.M.S. TOPAZE.

2 Above: Sardonyx cameo portrait of the Emperor Augustus (r. 27 BC–AD 14), from the collection of the Duc de Blacas. The collection, one of the finest of the 19th century, was begun by the Duke's father (d. 1834), French Ambassador to Rome and Naples. The Duke directed that on his death it be sold entire. The Museum acquired it for £48,000 in 1866 with the support of Benjamin Disraeli, then Chancellor of the Exchequer, and to the fury of Napoleon III. The cameo formerly belonged to Monsignor Leo Strozzi. *H. 12.8 cm*

3 Right: Brass ewer decorated in Mosul, AD 1232, in the workshop of Shuja' ibn Man'a, and acquired at the Blacas sale. The only extant inlaid brass vessel inscribed as being made in Mosul. A documentary piece and thus particularly favoured by the Museum. By purchase or gift (from himself or others such as John Henderson), A.W. Franks (p. 29) added more than 3,000 objects from the Islamic world to the handful previously in the Museum's collection. *H. 30.4 cm*

4 The 'Armada medal' of Queen Elizabeth I, made 1580–90, probably by the portrait miniaturist Nicholas Hilliard (1547–1619), and given as a gift from the Queen to a favoured courtier or political ally. From a collection of 4,347 historical medals purchased for £2,288 8s. 0d from Edward Hawkins (1780–1867), Keeper of Antiquities, in 1860. Hawkins holds the dubious distinction of having produced a scholarly catalogue which was destroyed by the Trustees on account of his freely expressed prejudices against historical figures. *H. 56 mm*

5 Henry Christy (1810–65), a successful businessman and traveller who introduced Turkish towelling into Britain. He was interested in the then fashionable investigation of parallels between prehistoric and tribal societies. A friend of A.W. Franks, in 1865 he bequeathed a collection of some 20,000 prehistoric and ethnographic objects, so vast that it had to remain in his flat in Victoria Street until space was available at Bloomsbury in the 1880s after the departure of natural history.

6 Christy bequeathed much of his collection to four Trustees, including A.W. Franks, who in 1865 transferred it to the Museum. The bequest included £5,000 which formed a substantial trust fund used for many years to acquire objects such as this unique Mixtec-Aztec turquoise mosaic of a double-headed serpent (*c.* AD 1500). *H. 20.5 cm*

7 The Museum forecourt, *c.* 1860. The Principal Librarian, the heads of department (Keepers) and their families lived on site. On summer evenings young ladies would promenade in the 'wrangle' and their parents would receive visitors.

8 Glass bottle in the shape of a leather pilgrim flask, probably made in Damascus during the second half of the 14th century, from the bequest of Felix Slade (1790–1868), which was valued at £28,000, and included 330 specimens of antique glass and 580 of Arab, Venetian and German glass. *H. 23 cm*

9 'Interior of our Tomb of Residence'. The Museum is particularly rich in Libyan antiquities thanks to excavations carried out from 1860–61 by Captain R. Murdoch Smith and Commander E.A. Porcher at Cyrene.

10 Marble statue of Apollo, 2nd century AD. Roman copy of a Hellenistic original of c. 200–150 BC, excavated in 121 fragments by R. Murdoch Smith at the Temple of Apollo, Cyrene, in 1861. H. 2.29 m

11 Below: Augustus Wollaston Franks (1826–97) who laid the foundations of many of today's Museum departments. He lavished his personal fortune on the Museum, giving around 7,000 objects prior to his great bequest. He became Keeper of British & Medieval Antiquities and Ethnography in 1866.

12 Left: The 'Franks casket', whalebone, made in Northumbria c. AD 700. Carved with scenes from Christian, Germanic and Roman tradition, it bears the longest runic text known on a portable object. The casket was used as a workbox in Auzon, Haute-Loire, France, and then emerged at a Paris dealer's. In 1858 the purchase of 'some Ancient carvings in ivory' for 100 guineas having been declined by the Trustees, it was bought privately by A.W. Franks. In 1867 he gave it to the Museum. L. 22.9 cm

'I have letters of introduction and a ticket of admission to the British Museum… The Museum library contains six hundred thousand volumes; the reading-room is vast, circular in form, and covered with a cupola, so that no one is far from the central office, and no one has the light in his eyes. All the lower stage of shelves is filled with works of reference – dictionaries, collections of biographies, classics of all sorts – which can be consulted on the spot, and are excellently arranged. Moreover, a small plan placed on each table indicates where they are placed and the order in which they stand. Each seat is isolated; there is nothing in front but the woodwork of the desk, so that no one is annoyed by the presence of his neighbour. The seats and the tables are covered with leather, and are very clean; there are two pens to each desk, the one being a steel, the other a quill pen; there is also a small stand at the side, upon which a second volume, or the volume from which extracts are being copied, may be placed. To procure a book, the title is written on a form, which is handed to the central office; the attendant brings the book to you himself, and does so without delay… For ladies a place is reserved, which is a delicate piece of attention.'
H. Taine, Notes on England, *trans. W.F. Rae (1872)*

1 The Reading Room in 1875. The photograph shows (foreground) the area most probably favoured by Karl Marx who last renewed his reader's ticket in November 1877. Among the revolutionaries who used the room were Plekhanov, Kropotkin, Vera Zasulich, Lenin and Trotsky.

2 Above: Afro-Portuguese ivory 'salt' cellar. From Benin, Nigeria, late 15th to early 16th century AD. Given by Major General Augustus Meyrick in 1878. Part of the collection of Samuel Rush Meyrick (1783–1848) which was particularly rich in European armour, initially offered to the Museum by his family but turned down by government. After the sale of the European section, the remainder was donated. *H. 43 cm*

3 Right: Cuneiform tablet bearing a 7th-century BC Akkadian account of a flood similar to that in the Bible. The significance of a fragment from the excavations of Layard and Rassam was realised in 1872 by George Smith (1840–76), an Assistant at the Museum. A further fragment was found by Smith at Nineveh on an expedition financed by the *Daily Telegraph*. Smith returned to the Near East for two further seasons and died in Aleppo in 1876. The Museum paid for a tombstone. *H. 15.24 cm*

4 The International Congress of Orientalists inspect the Rosetta Stone in 1874.

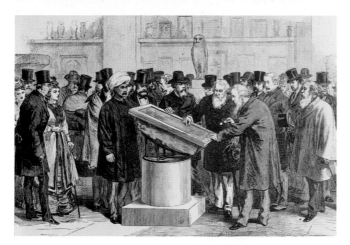

5 Right: Brass incense burner made in Damascus, Syria, AD 1277–79. The inscription includes the names and titles of an important Mamluk Amir Badr al-Din Baysari (d. 1298). From the superlative collection of 868 objects bequeathed by John Henderson (1797–1878) – one of the earliest collectors of Islamic art in Britain. *Diam 18.4 cm*

6 Below: Ganesha, 13th century AD, Orissa. From the collection of Indian sculpture given by the Bridge family in 1872. Previously displayed in a museum at their house in Shepherd's Bush, it consisted of around a hundred sculptures and eighty smaller objects, originally collected in India by Charles 'Hindoo' Stuart (1757/8–1828). *H. 1.02 m*

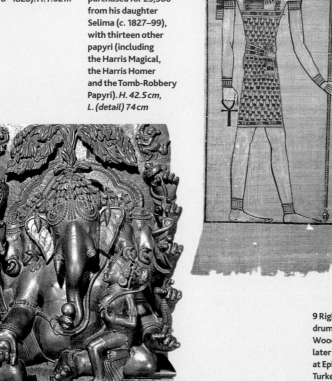

7 Right: The Great Harris Papyrus is one of the longest from Ancient Egypt (42 metres). This detail shows Ramesses III before the gods of Memphis: Ptah, Sekhmet and Nefertem. From Thebes, near Medinet Habu, *c*. 1200 BC. The papyrus was acquired by A.C. Harris (1790–1869) in 1854–5, and in 1872 purchased for £3,300 from his daughter Selima (*c*. 1827–99), with thirteen other papyri (including the Harris Magical, the Harris Homer and the Tomb-Robbery Papyri). *H. 42.5 cm, L. (detail) 74 cm*

9 Right: Marble column drum excavated by Wood in 1871 from the later temple of Artemis at Ephesos (modern Turkey), one of the Seven Wonders of the Ancient World, built *c*. 325–300 BC. *H. 1.84 m*

8 Right: J.T. Wood excavated at Ephesos 1863–74. Aiming to find the Temple of Artemis, he initially discovered only remains of the Roman and Byzantine city, but in 1866, funded by the Museum, he located the road leading to the sanctuary. This photograph (December 1871) shows Wood's excavations at the Temple.

'It is pleasant to go out again into the portico under the great columns. On the threshold I feel nearer knowledge than when within. The sun shines, and southwards above the houses there is a statue crowning the summit of some building… The green lawn is pleasant to look at, though it is mown so ruthlessly. If they would only let the grass spring up, there would be a thought somewhere entangled in the long blades as a dewdrop sparkles in their depths.

Seats should be placed here, under the great columns or by the grass, so that one might enjoy the sunshine after books and watch the pigeons. They have no fear of the people, they come to my feet, but the noise of a door heavily swinging-to in the great building alarms them; they rise and float round, and return again.'

Samuel J. Looker, Richard Jefferies' London *(1944)*, c. *1880*

1 Reindeer antler spear-thrower, approx. 12,500 years old. Purchased in 1887 from the railway engineer Peccadeau de l'Isle. In 1866 de l'Isle excavated the rock shelter of Montastruc, Tarn-et-Garonne and found some remarkable works of Old Stone Age art. The entire collection was acquired with the aid of the Christy Fund (p. 28). *L. 12.4 cm*

2 *Scenes in a Theatre Tea-house* (1685), Ukiyo-e ('floating world') handscroll painting by Hishikawa Moronobu (*c.* 1618–94). From a collection acquired in 1881 of 3,299 Japanese (and some Chinese) paintings formed by the British surgeon William Anderson (1842–1900), head of the naval medical college, Tokyo. 'Without this imaginative acquisition, it is doubtful whether the British Museum would have become, as it did, the national collection of Japanese painting, and the best in Europe in this field.' *31.5 x 147 cm*

3 Left: Porcelain 'Nabeshima' dish, 18th to 19th century AD, made at Okawachi near Arita for use at the sole discretion of the Nabeshima clan. Part of a collection of almost 3,500 pieces of oriental pottery and porcelain given by A. W. Franks in 1885. *Diam. 20.3 cm*

4 Below: Carillon clock, made *c.* 1589 by Isaac Habrecht (1544–1620). From the papal collections, it probably left Italy during the Napoleonic wars. Acquired by William I of the Netherlands. It was bought in London after 1848 by Octavius Morgan MP (1803–88). Morgan bequeathed 46 clocks, 238 watches and 84 watch movements. *H. 1.58 m*

5 The south-east corner of the Museum, *c.* 1900. In the foreground are staff residences, beyond is the White Wing fronting Montague Street. William White , a barrister (d. 1823), bequeathed around £72,000 for new buildings, received in 1879 on the death of his widow.

6 A Victorian family in front of the north-west gate from Nimrud. Restrictions on entry were relaxed in 1878. Babes in arms were now admitted, making it easier for poor families to visit.

7 Right: Pressure on space became insuperable and calls were made for the removal of the non-Classical collections. Plans for a Museum of Natural History were approved in February 1871. The first objects left in 1880, the last in 1883. A verse in *Punch* proclaimed 'Out with weazles, ferrets, skunks… Here, in future, folks shall scan Nothing but the works of Man'.

8 Coffin bearing the words 'Artemidorus, farewell!', with a painted wax portrait of its occupant, a young Graeco-Egyptian who died *c*. AD 100–120. Found by the archaeologist W.M. Flinders Petrie at Hawara in 1888. Petrie wrote in his journal of a 'procession of three gilt mummies… seen coming across the mounds, glittering in the sun'. Given by Henry Martyn Kennard. *H. 1.71 m*

10 Below: Glass drinking vessel, early 7th century AD, from a group of four found in the grave of an Anglo-Saxon chieftain at Taplow. The grave also contained gold buckles, a bronze bowl, drinking horns, bone gaming pieces, the remains of a lyre and gold braids from a rich cloak. Given by the Revd Charles Whateley, Rector of Taplow, in 1883. *H. 30.1 cm*

9 Above: Drum slab depicting the Great Buddhist Stupa at Amaravati, Deccan, India, 3rd century AD. The stupa, 1st to 3rd century AD, was found in 1797 by Colonel Colin Mackenzie, recorded by him in 1816 and excavated by Sir Walter Elliot in 1845. Some 121 sculptures were sent to London in 1859 but much remains in Madras. On the dispersal of the India Office Museum in 1880, the Museum received the Amaravati sculptures and other items. Some material went to the V&A. *H. 1.24 m*

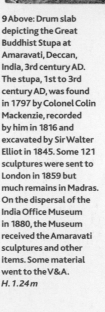

11 Right: Excavation at Taplow, Buckinghamshire, in 1883, of the richest Anglo-Saxon grave found in England prior to Sutton Hoo (p. 45). The find should have been more spectacular but the weight of the earth had crushed some objects and additional damage was caused by the fall of an old yew tree.

'As the visitor to the British Museum gazes upon the ancient vellum of the Codex Alexandrinus and recalls that some fourteen hundred years have passed away since it was written, or stands in front of the Theseus of the Elgin Marbles and realizes that the sculptor who fashioned that stone has been in his grave over two thousand three hundred years, he will surely confess to a feeling that here indeed are objects which dwarf his own three-score-years-and-ten and make young again many a relic which he deemed venerable. And yet that manuscript and that marble are modern and almost contemporaneous compared with the relics of old Egypt.

No wonder, then, that Egyptology is as catching as measles. It is also as instructive as orchid hunting.'
Henry C. Shelley, The British Museum: Its History and Treasures *(1899)*

2 Above: Pottery bowl (*krater*), Mycenaean, *c.* 1300–1200 BC, found in a tomb at Enkomi. In the 1890s the Museum carried out excavations in Cyprus, funded with a bequest from Miss Emma Turner. *H. 27.2 cm*

1 Experiments with electricity had begun in the Reading Room in 1879. In 1890 the exhibition galleries were lit by electric light and the public no longer had to leave when it got dark. On 8 February 1890 a private view of the new lighting was held.

3 The Holy Thorn reliquary, made *c.* 1400–10 for the Duc de Berry. It was bequeathed by Baron Ferdinand de Rothschild (1839–98) as part of a collection of 256 items: 'plate, enamels, bijouterie carvings in boxwood, majolica, glass, arms and armour' valued at £325,000, displayed in the 'new smoking room' at his home at Waddesdon Manor, Buckinghamshire, a great princely treasure house in the continental European tradition. *H. 30.5 cm*

4 Mounted fan entitled 'The Garden', 1741, from the collection of 687 fans, fan leaves and playing cards given by Lady Charlotte Schreiber. Her son wrote of her 'she left no stone unturned, no difficulty, discomfort, fatigue, or hardship of travel daunted her'.

5 Lady Charlotte Schreiber (1812–95), one of the first to take a scholarly interest in pottery and porcelain. Lady Charlotte married an iron magnate, managed the Dowlais iron works after his death and then, to her family's dismay, married her children's tutor. From the age of fifty she was an indefatigable collector, particularly of china.

6 Gold dinara coin of Kumaragupta I, north India, *c.* AD 415–50, from General Sir Alexander Cunningham's collection of 5,017 oriental coins. The greater part was purchased in 1888–94. Cunningham (1814–93), who was Director-General of the Indian Archaeological Survey 1871–85, also bequeathed 2,142 coins 'quite unrivalled both in content and completeness in this particular series by any other collection public or private'. *Diam. 20 mm*

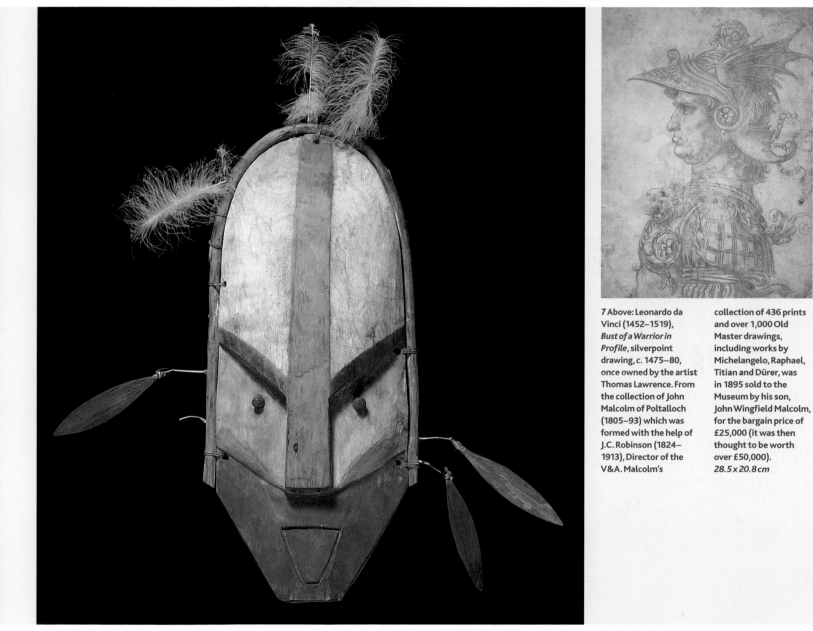

7 Above: Leonardo da Vinci (1452–1519), *Bust of a Warrior in Profile*, silverpoint drawing, *c.* 1475–80, once owned by the artist Thomas Lawrence. From the collection of John Malcolm of Poltalloch (1805–93) which was formed with the help of J.C. Robinson (1824–1913), Director of the V&A. Malcolm's collection of 436 prints and over 1,000 Old Master drawings, including works by Michelangelo, Raphael, Titian and Dürer, was in 1895 sold to the Museum by his son, John Wingfield Malcolm, for the bargain price of £25,000 (it was then thought to be worth over £50,000). *28.5 x 20.8 cm*

8 Above: Alutiiq mask probably from Alaska (Kodiak or at Katmai), from the collection of about 200 items made by the 5th Earl of Lonsdale during his expedition of 1888–9 to north-west Canada and Alaska. *H. 46 cm*

9 Late Neolithic limestone 'drums', *c.* 2600–2000 BC, found in a child's grave at Folkton, Yorkshire: '3 very remarkable objects made of chalk, richly ornamented, and of unknown use'. Given in 1893 by Canon Greenwell of Durham Cathedral (1820–1918) and among a number of gifts made by him. In 1908 J. Pierpont Morgan purchased Greenwell's collection of 2,500 prehistoric bronze implements for £10,000 and gave them to the Museum. *H. 10.7 cm (max.)*

10 Right: Rock crystal skull purchased from Tiffany's, New York, in 1897 for $1,000, and said to have been acquired by a Spanish officer prior to the French occupation of Mexico in 1862–7. It is now thought that it is not Aztec but of more recent manufacture. It was previously in the collection of Eugène Boban, a French antiques dealer who had shops in Paris and Mexico City. *H. 25 cm*

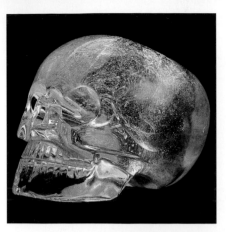

11 Below: Bracelet or armlet from the Oxus treasure, mainly 5th and 4th centuries BC, of which the Museum now has some 170 pieces. Thought to have been discovered on the north side of the River Oxus (present Amu dar'ya), at or close to Takht-i Kuwad (in modern Tadjikistan), between 1876 and 1880, it was bought by merchants, carried off by bandits, rescued by a British officer, dispersed in the bazaars of Rawalpindi and eventually much of it was acquired by A.W. Franks and General Sir Alexander Cunningham (who sold his collection to Franks). It formed part of Franks's immense bequest in 1897. *H. 12.3 cm*

12 Above: 'Burnet Rose', a collage of coloured paper cut by Mrs Mary Delany (1700–88) who began these intricate works when she was aged seventy-two and completed nearly 1,000 before failing eyesight obliged her to stop ten years later. Bequeathed by her great-great niece Lady Llanover in 1896. *24.3 x 20.3 cm*

13 Left: The Royal Gold Cup of the sovereigns of France and England, made for the Duc de Berry (1340–1416) *c.* 1380, which passed to the English Crown through John, Duke of Bedford. Given to the Spanish envoy by James I in 1604, it was in 1610 presented to the convent of Santa Clara at Medina de Pomar. In 1883 it was bought for £100 by Baron Jerome Pichon, a noted Parisian collector who subsequently sold it to the dealer Wertheimer for £8,000. The Museum bought it at cost price in 1892, the cost being met by a private subscription organised by A.W. Franks. *H. 23.6 cm*

14 Brass plaque from Benin (now Nigeria), 16th century AD. In 1897, following an attack on a British consular mission, a British punitive expedition took Benin City. There they found the royal palace being rebuilt. Some 900 plaques from the old building were discovered half buried in a storehouse. *H. 38.5 cm*

'The British Museum is the history of the world: in its Bloomsbury galleries the history of civilization, in its Cromwell Road galleries the history of nature; in Bloomsbury man, in Cromwell Road God. The lesson of the British Museum is the transitoriness of man and the littleness of his greatest deeds. That is the burden of its every Bloomsbury room. The ghosts of dead peoples, once dominant, inhabit it; the dust of empires fills its air. One may turn in from Oxford Street and in half an hour pass all the nations of the earth, commanding and servile, cultured and uncouth, under review. The finest achievements of Greek Sculpture are here, and here are the painted canoes of the South Sea islander; the Egyptian Book of the Dead is here, and here, in the Reading Room, is a copy of the work you are now judiciously skipping; the obelisk of Shalmaneser is here... It is not until one has wandered in the British Museum for some weeks that one begins to realise how inexhaustible it is. To know it is impossible; but the task of extracting its secrets is made less difficult by acquiring and studying its excellent catalogues, which are on sale in the Entrance Hall.'

E.V. Lucas, A Wanderer in London *(1906)*

1 Naturally preserved body of a man, late Predynastic period, c. 3400 BC, from Gebelein, Egypt. It arrived on a Friday in March 1900 and by Monday the Keeper of Egyptian Antiquities reported that a fingertip had mysteriously disappeared. This was found during a recent examination, clutched tightly in the fist. L. 1.63 m

2 Left: The first of many hundreds of gifts to the Museum by the National Art Collections Fund (NACF) was made in 1904, an English repeating watch made by Daniel Quare, c. 1705–15, given through the Fund by Max Rosenheim (p. 61). The NACF was founded in 1903 'to help secure works of art of all periods for the museums and galleries of this country and the Commonwealth, by gift, bequest or purchase'. Diam. (of case) 55 mm

3 'Dusters', c. 1905–10. An earlier member of this grade was Henry Hooke who was awarded the Victoria Cross after the siege of Rorke's Drift.

4 1906 cartoon suggesting ways of popularising the Museum in response to a newspaper report that attendances were falling off. The departure of natural history had led to a drop in visitor numbers, but in 1901 the total again exceeded that of 1880–3. There were 691,950 visitors in 1906.

5 Below: Detail of a Mexican screenfold book, the Codex Zouche-Nuttall, Mixtec, AD 1200–1521. One of the few to have survived, it emerged in a Dominican monastery in Florence in 1859. Some years later, Sir Robert Curzon, 14th Baron Zouche (1810–73) loaned it to the Museum. It was published by Zelia Nuttall in 1902. Curzon's sister, Baroness Zouche of Haryngworth, in 1917 bequeathed the codex as part of a collection of 91 western and 103 oriental manuscripts, 43 printed books and some prints. *19 x 113.5 cm*

6 Painting on silk of the Bodhisattva Avalokitesvara, from Dunhuang, China, AD 910. Sir Aurel Stein (1862–1942) led three expeditions to Central Asia between 1900 and 1915. In 1907, during his second, jointly financed by the Museum and the Government of India, he found at the 1,000 Buddha Caves near Dunhuang in Gansu Province, western China, thousands of silk paintings and manuscripts on paper, hidden for almost a millennium. Stein removed scrolls and other materials in return for contributions to the renovation of temples. *H. 77 cm*

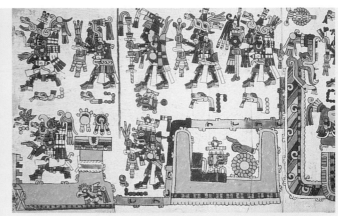

7 Statues of Senwosret III, *c.* 1850 BC, from Deir el-Bahari, Thebes. Among many continuing gifts made by the Egypt Exploration Fund (now Society). The Fund was founded in 1882 by Amelia Edwards and Erasmus Wilson, together with scholars from the Museum's Department of Coins and Medals, somewhat with the disapproval of the Keeper of Oriental Antiquities. The first British body to undertake regular excavations in Egypt, it continues to carry out research. *H. 1.42 m*

8 The finder of the Croydon hoard of Roman coins in 1903. A selection of 210 coins was given to the Museum by Croydon Town Council. Throughout the 19th and early 20th centuries many coin hoards and other antiquities were unearthed by engineering and other works, and chance discoveries continue.

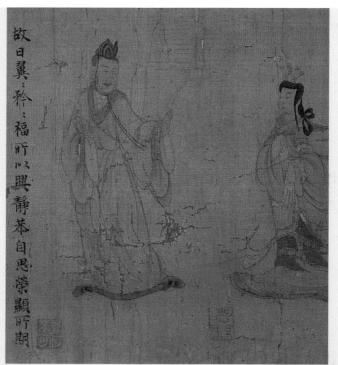

9 Left: Detail of a Chinese scroll painting, *Admonitions of the Instructress to the Court Ladies*, executed in the tradition of the early Chinese artist Gu Kaizhi (*c.* AD 345–406). At one time thought to be a Tang dynasty copy (AD 618–907), it is now considered by some scholars to be earlier. Before its arrival in the Museum, the scroll passed through many hands, the first owner's seal dating to the 8th century. It entered the imperial collection during the reign of the Qianlong emperor. *25 x 348 cm (total length)*

10 Right: Buddhist reliquary made of gold set with garnets, from Bimaran stupa 2, Afghanistan, *c.* 1st century AD. Excavated in 1834 by Charles Masson (alias James Lewis, 1800–53), 'adventurer, spy and writer of bad verse', it is amongst the earliest representations of the Buddha in the art of greater India. About 250 Masson coins came to the Museum with 2,430 transferred by the India Office in 1882, and about 6,000 with the 10,000 residue of the India Office collection loaned by the British Library in 1995. Manuscript records are today being studied to reconstruct the archaeological record of the sites Masson explored. *H. 6.7 cm*

11 Above: Wooden statue (*ndop*) of Shyaam aMbul aNgoong, 17th-century founder of the Kuba Kingdom, Congo, probably late 18th century, given to Emil Torday in 1909 by King Kwete Peshanga Kena. The 3,000 items Torday collected form one of the best documented early collections from Africa. *H. 54.5 cm*

12 Left: Long-term project for expanding outwards from the Smirke core proposed by the architect J.J. Burnet (viewed from the south-east). With the ending of the Boer War in 1902, government funds were available to match a £150,000 legacy from Vincent Stuckey Lean (1820–99) for the construction of the northern wing (King Edward VII's Galleries) on land purchased from the Bedford Estates in 1894–5 – the only section completed.

'In the Bloomsbury Museum are stored the records of all that most definitely distinguishes man from other animals. It guards and preserves the history of the human soul. All the long endeavour of mankind to express itself in forms of beauty is there to be traced in type through the undated ages of man's existence, from the scratches upon stag-horns or the ivory of mammoths up to the arts of Egypt and Assyria, the Athenian marbles and vases, the Roman bronzes, the variegated splendours of the East, and Europe's decisive purity of form. There are preserved the inscriptions which have opened shafts of light into the dark abysses of the past. There is the great Library in which are kept alive rather than embalmed the thoughts and actions of the human race, the efforts to express in words the soul's deepest emotions and desires; the efforts to pass beyond the flaming ramparts of the world, or to leave some record of the struggles which have marked man's growth, the joys and sorrows which have befallen him upon the way.' The Nation, *12 January 1918*

1 J.M.W. Turner (1775–1851), *Vale of Ashburnham* (East Sussex), 1816, from the bequest by George Salting (1835–1909) of 433 prints and drawings including eighteen Turners. Son of a Danish merchant who had made a fortune in Australia, Salting, who had wide interests and an income of around £30,000 a year, was described by *The Times* on his death as 'the greatest English art-collector of this age, perhaps of any age'. *38 x 56.4 cm*

2 Above: Gold tanka of Sultan Qutb al-Din Mubarak Shah (1316–20), of Delhi, India, from the collection of Muhammadan coins formed by George Bleazby, presented in 1911 by Henry Van den Bergh to commemorate the Delhi durbar. *Diam. 23 mm*

3 From 1915, during the First World War, sculptures were protected *in situ* by sandbags or removed to the basements. Because of the danger of air raids, early in 1918 the most portable objects of special value were transferred to the Postal Tube Railway at Holborn. Other material went to the National Library of Wales at Aberystwyth and to a country house near Malvern.

4 Right: T.E. Lawrence (of Arabia) (1888–1935) at the excavations funded by the Museum at Carchemish, south-east Anatolia, which took place 1911–14, more than coincidentally near the route of the Berlin–Baghdad railway. D.G. Hogarth and Leonard Woolley were also involved.

5 Right: Basalt lion head, 9th century BC, from the excavations of the Neo-Hittite site at Carchemish. Part of a base of two lions held by an attendant that was smashed by looters during the First World War, the fragment was acquired in 1927. *H. 48 cm*

6 Left: Opening of King Edward VII's Galleries by King George V and Queen Mary on 7 May 1914. The popular papers were preoccupied by the first appearance of Princess Mary (inset) with her hair up. The Galleries were designed by Sir J.J. Burnet (p. 39) and built at a cost of £200,000.

7 Left: Louhan (a Buddhist saint or wise man who has attained nirvana) from Yixian, Hebei Province, China, AD 907–1125. The Keeper, having been invited to see it by a dealer, 'at once determined to make an effort to secure it'. The special price of £5,000 (at least half its probable value) was largely funded by private subscription, including £1,000 from the NACF. *H. 1.3 m*

8 Left: Head of the Roman Emperor Augustus (r. 27 BC–AD 14), found by Professor John Garstang during excavations at Meroë in the Sudan in 1910, 'hidden by design in a pocket of soft sand'. It may have come from a statue in Roman Egypt decapitated by Meroitic tribesmen and taken beyond the imperial frontier. Presented by the Sudan Excavation Committee in return for £1,050 for their excavations given by the NACF. *H. 47.75 cm*

9 Above: Print of the Kabuki actors Nakamura Wadaemon and Nakamura Konozō by Tōshūsai Sharaku, 1794, given by Sir Ernest Satow (1843–1929), British Minister to Japan and later China. In 1884 and 1885 he gave around 1,000 volumes of Japanese books. *35 x 24.2 cm*

10 Right: Statue of A'a from Rurutu, Austral Islands, late 18th century, given to the London Missionary Society in 1821 as a symbol of the islanders' acceptance of Christianity. Part of a collection of around 240 objects sold to the Museum in 1911 on condition that the Society's name should be attached to it. *H. 1.17 m*

'I made my first visit to the British Museum in 1921 when I came to London from Yorkshire with a scholarship to the Royal College of Art. The Museum was a revelation to me. I went at least twice a week for two or three hours each time, and one room after another caught my enthusiasm. The wonderful thing about the British Museum is that everything is stretched out before you and you are free to make your own discoveries… In my most formative years, nine-tenths of my understanding and learning about sculpture came from the British Museum… Until I came to London the only real sculptures which I had seen (apart from plaster casts in art school) were the Gothic heads on the porch of Methley Church, two miles from my birth town Castleford, so when I first visited the British Museum's Egyptian sculpture gallery, and saw the 'great arm' and imagined what the whole figure was like, which it had only been part of, then I realised how monumental, how enormous, how impressive a single piece of sculpture could be.'

Henry Moore, Henry Moore at the British Museum *(1981)*

1 Michelangelo Buonarroti (1475–1564), study for the figure of Adam in *The Creation of Man* on the ceiling of the Sistine Chapel, *c.* 1511. Given by the NACF in 1926, with contributions from Joseph Duveen and Henry van den Bergh. Previous owners include the artists Thomas Lawrence and Joshua Reynolds. *19.3 x 25.9 cm*

3 Below: Stone bust representing a personification of the young Maize god from Copán, Honduras, Maya, AD 300–600. Given to the V&A by Alfred Maudslay in 1886 and later transferred to the British Museum. *H. 90 cm*

2 Right: Alfred Percival Maudslay (1850–1931): 'Chichén Itzá. My room, 1889'. Maudslay made eight pioneering expeditions to Maya lands from 1881 to 1894. His collection of moulds of Maya sculptures, made of paper squeezes or plaster, was given to the V&A and casts were made in 1886–91. Over 400 plaster casts were in 1922 transferred to the British Museum and some were displayed in the first room to be named after a living donor. From Maudslay also came nine stone sculptures from Copán (Honduras) and eight lintels from Yaxchilán (Mexico).

4 Left: On the return of antiquities from wartime storage in 1919, some objects had suffered deterioration because of the environments in which they were kept. A temporary conservation laboratory was set up in May 1920 under Dr Alexander Scott (1853–1947), and became a permanent department of the Museum in 1931.

5 Excavations at Ur, southern Mesopotamia (Iraq), conducted by Sir Leonard Woolley, took place between 1922 and 1934. From 1927 onwards a unique Sumerian cemetery, c. 2600 BC, of unparalleled richness and variety and with hundreds of graves, was uncovered. Sixteen tombs each contained a number of bodies including sacrificed retainers. Deep excavations as seen here revealed prehistoric layers, the earliest of which date to the Al' Ubaid period (c. 5900/5500 BC to 4000 BC).

6 The 'Ram in the thicket' – the figure of a male goat made of gold, shell and lapis lazuli, from the 'Great Death pit' within the Royal cemetery at Ur, Mesopotamia, c. 2600 BC. One of a pair, the statue was so named by the excavator, Leonard Woolley, who liked the biblical allusion to Genesis 22:13. H. 45.7 cm

7 Above: Alfred Hitchcock's first talking picture, Blackmail (1929), was partly filmed in the upper Egyptian galleries.

In 1923 the Museum attracted over 1 million visitors – the first occasion since the Great Exhibition of 1851.

8 Late Celtic bronze mirror, 50 BC–AD 50, found at Desborough, Northamptonshire, in 1808, during excavations for ironstone. The Desborough Museum was given first refusal and when it was unable to complete the purchase the mirror was in 1924 acquired by the NACF and given to the British Museum. L. 35 cm

9 Right: Pair of carved wooden doors from the Palace of the Ogoga Ekere Ikiti, eastern Yorubaland, carved by Olowe of Ise and acquired in 1920 in exchange for a specially made throne. H. 2.13 m

10 Right: The Museum galleries in 1922. Tourist: 'Come on Maria; we shall never get through if you stop looking at things.'

'There was a time when a visit to the British Museum would have been regarded as the driest of all dry ways of passing the time on a wet day. A few learned folk might gather there to look at the objects exhibited, some of the general public might go there to gaze at the memorials of a long forgotten past, and to wonder at the strange things they saw, or to stare at the mummies brought from Egypt, but to the great bulk of the population of London, the whole thing was as dry as the mummies themselves.

To-day there is an entirely different feeling about it, and a visit will show that thousands of people find it a place of real interest, for in summer, as well as in winter, a goodly number can always be found wandering round the various galleries, examining the exhibits, or listening to guides, official or private, who point out the things to be seen, and indicate their bearing upon history, religion, philosophy and science.'
W.H. Boulton, The Romance of the British Museum *(1931)*

1 Yoruba cast brass head of a ruler, from Ife, south Nigeria, 12th to 14th century AD, one of a number found in 1938 during building operations. Acquired by the NACF and given to the Museum. A contemporary report notes: 'Of great interest as an ethnographic object, it was even more striking as a work of art'. H. 35 cm

2 Queen Mary and the Princesses Elizabeth and Margaret Rose, on a visit to the Museum in 1937, being shown the Rosetta Stone by the Director, Sir John Forsdyke. The *Illustrated London News* noted that the few members of the public in the building were mostly unaware of their presence.

3 Marble figure of the Buddha Amitabha, from Chongguang temple, Hancui village, Hebei, northern China, Sui dynasty, AD 585. Presented by C.T. Loo to the Chinese government and by them to the Museum in 1938, to commemorate the International Exhibition of Chinese Art in London, 1935–6, 'as a token of the good will existing between our two peoples'. H. 5.8 m

4 Right: Planning for the evacuation of the collections in the event of a future war began in 1933. Packing lists were compiled and out-of-town repositories sought. Thousands of collapsible boxes were stored under the new Gallery being constructed for the Parthenon sculptures

with funds provided by Sir Joseph Duveen. Once the boxes were assembled and filled with objects they could be loaded into containers for transport to a railway station. They were then taken by rail to their destination, offloaded and taken by lorry to the repository.

5 Right: The evacuation of objects began on 24 August 1939, the day after the signing of the Nazi–Soviet pact. Within two weeks the most portable and valuable items had gone to Boughton and Drayton houses in Northamptonshire, the National Library of Wales and the Aldwych tube tunnel. Dispersal continued throughout the war.

6 Right: Bronze double-ram *zun* (ritual wine vessel), Shang period, China, 13th to 12th century BC, possibly from Hunan, purchased from George Eumorfopoulos (1863–1939). Although he had intended to make a bequest to the nation, because of the trade depression he was obliged in 1931 to sell his Chinese collection to the Museum and the V&A, but at the very generous price of £100,000, well under half its market value. The Eumorfopoulos collection of Chinese antiquities was described as the most extensive and best chosen of all the great private collections being built up in the first part of the 20th century. *H. 43.2 cm*

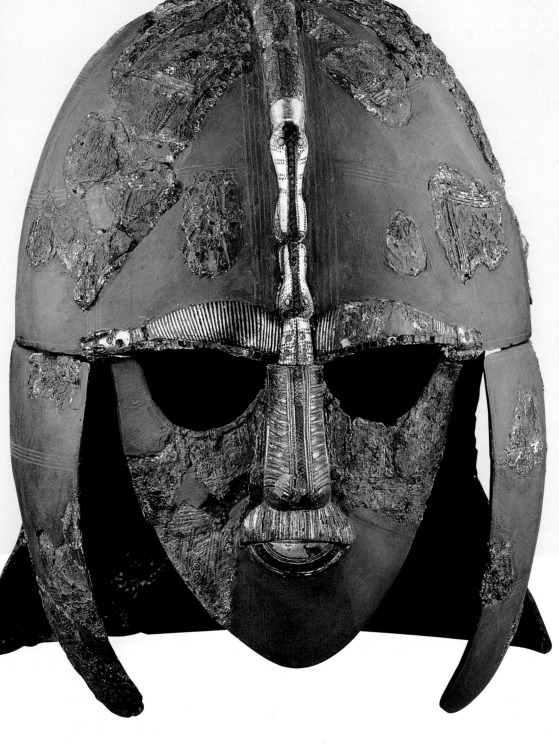

7 Below: Reconstructed helmet from the Sutton Hoo ship-burial. It was initially assumed that the burial was an empty grave as no trace of a body could be found. Phosphate deposits discovered during excavations in 1967 indicate that a king was most probably buried there, possibly Raedwald (AD 590–625/6), overlord of the English kingdoms between 616 and his death. *H. 31.8 cm*

8 Above: In 1939 the burial site of a magnificent Anglo-Saxon ship, nearly 30 metres long, was found at Sutton Hoo, Suffolk. Mrs Pretty (1883–1942), the landowner who gave the treasure to the Museum, watches Stuart Piggott, W.F. Grimes, Sir John Forsdyke (Director of the British Museum) and T.D. Kendrick (Keeper of British & Medieval Antiquities) examining the garnet and gold shoulder clasps found in the burial. The treasure was placed in the Aldwych tube tunnel for safekeeping during the War.

9 Bronze cat from Memphis or Saqqara, Egypt, *c.* 664–332 BC, offered by John Gayer-Anderson Pasha in 1939, subject to a life interest by Mary Stout, which came to the Museum after the Second World War. *H. 42 cm*

'We went down about sixty feet into a dark place, until we were halted by a fire-proof, steel door. We rang a bell and waited. In a minute or so we heard slow footsteps coming up an incline, then the sound of many withdrawn bolts and the click of a key in the lock. We entered a tunnel that descended at a steep angle still further into the earth. We then passed into a large vault, well lit with electric light and piled to the roof with crates and boxes, most of them stained a dark green colour. I have no idea how many there were. I should think there were thousands, one on top of the other, in great ramparts, with passage-ways between... "How deep down are we?" I asked. "Eighty feet below the pavement," replied my guide, "the safest spot in London." And I turned to examine the boxes, which contain some of the most priceless treasures of the British Museum: Egyptian gods, Greek bronzes, Etruscan metalwork, marble statues of Pharaoh and Caesar, Roman rings, and gold and alabaster vases from ancient tombs – the most amazing Aladdin's Cave ever seen.'

H.V. Morton, 'London in Wartime: Your Buried Treasure', 17 April 1940

1 On 10/11 May 1941 a stick of incendiaries ignited roofs in the south-west corner of the site; the Coin Room was destroyed and about 250,000 books were lost in the burnt out south-west book stack. For some time after the end of the War, umbrellas had to be carried in this area of the Museum but the Director's children greatly enjoyed playing on the 'stepping stones'.

2 Below: One of the most important surviving sets of late Roman silver tableware, the 4th-century AD thirty-four-piece Mildenhall treasure found in Suffolk in 1942 by a tractor driver ploughing a field. Acquired by the Museum as treasure trove in 1946. Although its value was estimated at £20,000, a considerably reduced award was paid because it was not initially reported to the authorities. *Diam. (of Great Dish) 60.5 cm*

3 The chi-rho monogram (the first letters of Christ's name in Greek) from a series of Christian wall paintings, 4th century AD, found on the site of a late Roman villa at Lullingstone, Kent, in 1949. Given by Kent County Council in 1967. *Diam. (of roundel) 90 cm*

4 Right: The largest surviving tile pavement from a medieval private house comes from a house in Redcliffe Street, Bristol, that had previously belonged to William Canynges, a wealthy merchant and Lord Mayor (d. 1474). Probably made c. 1481–1515, it was removed in 1913. Part of a collection of over 8,000 tiles bought from the Duke of Rutland in 1947 for £6,000 with a contribution from the NACF. Built up since the 1840s, the Museum's collection of over 15,000 tiles includes almost every known type of decoration.

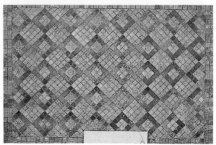

5 Left: Inspecting the Museum's collections stored in the Westwood quarry near Bradford on Avon. In 1942, the Prime Minister having used his influence, objects were moved from Boughton and Drayton, both now close to an airfield, to this secret underground quarry. Housing priceless objects from other museums and private individuals, this became one of the richest treasure caves of all time.

6 Egyptian antiquities stored in the Great Hall at Boughton House, Northamptonshire, in December 1941. During the 'phoney war', many of the staff were dispersed either to the repositories or to war work, including Bletchley Park. In August 1940 a 'suicide exhibition' of graphics and duplicates which the Museum was prepared to lose was mounted at the top of the main stairs.

7 Right: Asante royal 'Kente' type cloth, made of woven silk, from Nsuta, Ghana. Purchased 1947. The Museum has a particularly fine collection of textiles from all over the world.

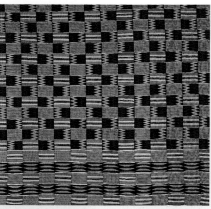

8 Left: Odilon Redon (1840–1916), La Cellule d'Or, 1892, from a bequest of more than 5,000 prints and drawings made by Campbell Dodgson (1867–1948), Keeper of Prints & Drawings from 1912 to 1932. He concentrated on work of the second half of the 19th century onwards, intending to bequeath the collection from the outset, as a complement to his Department's existing holdings. 30.1 x 24.7 cm

9 Above: The Portland Vase, the finest surviving example of Roman cameo glass, named after the Dukes of Portland who owned it from 1785 to 1945. Probably made in Italy c. AD 5–25. It was recorded in 1601, acquired by the Barberini family and in 1778 bought by Sir William Hamilton (p. 10) who sold it to the Portlands. In 1810 it was loaned to the Museum where it survived near destruction by an Irish student in 1845. Put up for sale at Christie's in 1929–32, it failed to reach its reserve price. It was bought by the Museum from the 7th Duke of Portland in 1945 for £5,000, with the aid of a bequest from James Rose Vallentin made in 1931. H. 24.5 cm

10 Right: Persian miniature painting from the Demotte Shah-nama (Book of Kings) of Firdausi, Tabriz, c. 1335, named after the dealer who sold the pages separately. In 1948 Sir Bernard Eckstein bequeathed 'a selection not exceeding thirty from my collection of Persian mss and miniatures' plus pieces of porcelain. H. (of page) 40.7 cm x W. 29.6 cm

'The devotion and care of those who packed and despatched the Manuscripts of the Royal Music Library during the war was rewarded on November 27th, when Her Majesty celebrated the Centenary of King George II's gift to the museum by a further gift of the Handel volumes… The Museum we must admit did itself (and we hope its Royal Visitor) proud. Its translation, as we know to our cost, those of us who picked our way for week after week through what was once the King's Library, but was for long unrecognisable under a vaulting of scaffolding, with wet wax below, before, everywhere; with Keepers incongruously poised on top of glass cases doing something to the lighting; with dust sheets, vociferous workmen, and a flood which threatened to drown a Roman Venus; new gratings, so that we cannot imagine pennies down below; this utter dislocation was of no consequence when we ascended the magic carpet, through the fairylike awning to enter the Hall, unusual and beautiful in its banks of flowers and after all, one is not received every day, by the Archbishop of Canterbury, the Lord Chancellor and the Speaker of the House of Commons. The golden curtaining of the Manuscript Saloon was the last touch of enchantment, till Her Majesty arrived.'
J. Quilter, Under the Dome, *December 1957*

1 Children at the entrance to the Mummy Room, 1954. By 1953, the Museum's 200th anniversary, many of the galleries had been restored after war damage, but much remained to be done. The anniversary itself was celebrated by a dinner in the unreconstructed Assyrian basement.

2 Above: *Seaport with the embarkation of St Paula*, from the *Liber Veritatis* of Claude Lorrain (c. 1604/5–82), begun c. 1635, which contains 195 drawings recording the paintings he had made throughout his career. The Museum has the largest collection of drawings by Claude in the world. The *Liber Veritatis* was in the collection of the Dukes of Devonshire by 1728. Accepted in lieu of Estate Duty after the death of the 9th Duke and allocated to the Museum in 1957. *26.3 x 19.9 cm*

4 Above: Between 1949 and 1958 Max Mallowan, husband of Agatha Christie, excavated at Nimrud for the British School of Archaeology in Iraq. This ivory panel of a lioness attacking an African boy, 9th to 8th century BC, was discovered in 1953 at the bottom of a well in the palace of the Assyrian king Ashurnasirpal II (r. 883–859 BC). It had probably been thrown there during the destruction of the palace in the late 7th century BC. Purchased from the British School of Archaeology in Iraq in 1954 for a £1,000 contribution to the excavation funds; a similar piece remained in Iraq. *L. 10.35 cm*

3 Right: The Lycurgus cup, probably made in Rome, 4th century AD. The red/green cup is the only complete example of a type of glass known as 'dichroic', which changes colour when held up to the light. Its existence was first recorded in 1845. Bought for £20,000 in 1958 with the assistance of the NACF. *H. 15.9 cm*

5 'Buzz off! The British Museum may be broke, but it's not as broke as all that.' A 1954 cartoon in the *Evening News* by Lee, showing a rag-and-bone man touting for business, announces that the Museum is yet again short of funds.

6 Left: Marine chronometer No. 12 by John Arnold, London, c. 1778–9, from the Ilbert collection. The collection was formed to demonstrate all aspects of the history of horology and transformed the Museum's holdings of this material into the best in the world. *H. (of box) 8.4 cm*

7 Right: Courtney Adrian Ilbert (1888–1957) formed a collection of approx. 2,300 watches and watch movements, 40 marine chronometers, 210 clocks, and various items of horological interest. Gilbert Edgar bought the clocks for the Museum for £50,000, and the Clockmakers Company arranged a £16,000 appeal to acquire the watches.

8 Igbo tiered sculpture which incorporates images of power, such as horsemen, military insignia, rifles and wild beasts. Such works act as the rallying points of different groups at public displays of dancing. Part of a collection of over 15,000 ethnographical objects collected by Sir Henry Wellcome (1853–1936) and given to the Museum in 1954 by the Trustees of the Wellcome Historical Medical Museum – 'the largest single acquisition [it] ever made'. *H. 1.5 m*

9 Above: Bronze head of Apollo, c. 460 BC, found at Tamassos, Cyprus in 1836. From the collection of the Dukes of Devonshire at Chatsworth House, Derbyshire. It was at Chatsworth for many years, unnoticed, until c. 1896 it was recognised as a rare Greek original. Given by the Treasury in 1958. *H. 31.6 cm*

10 Left: Dame Kathleen Kenyon, granddaughter of the 19th-century Keeper of Antiquities Edward Hawkins, and daughter of the Principal Librarian Sir Frederic Kenyon, excavated at Jericho 1952–8 for the British School of Archaeology in Jerusalem. Among the finds in 1954 was the Neolithic 'Jericho' skull, c. 7000 BC, one of several plastered skulls found beneath the floors of houses. *H. 20.3 cm*

'We last left you, if you remember, pondering at the bottom of the stairs whether you dare go up. Two wooden huts at the foot of them and scaffolding and tarpaulins blotting out the first landing suggests not. Take heart and go up there, you are only one of at least a million people who will have faced this problem this year...

Quickly one turns to the Museum's forte, the Upper Egyptian Galleries... The Museum reaches grisly and magnificent heights here... The fairground gaiety of the mummy cases, the bitter dark of their contents, the touching belief in corporeal survival, the blind, mute, suffocated dead in their wrappings, the romance of their discovery, have inspired the Museum into making their best casing and labelling efforts. It is a place in which to celebrate the deaths of others, safely contained in hermetically sealed glass...

The gentle cry of "Closing down now" starts to run through the galleries, and having been thrown out of some of the world's best museums I can verify it is never more pleasingly done than in Bloomsbury.

"Whoops, sorry", apologises a visitor to a lectern-like object standing in one of the aisles along which we are all fleeing. It is unlabelled from the rear and as she turns to see what it is a look of shock crosses her face. It is only the Rosetta Stone.'
Anne Sharpley, 'Playing the guessing game at the British Museum', Evening Standard, *29 June 1966*

1 Bronze head of the Emperor Claudius (r. AD 41–54), 1st century AD, found in the River Alde at Rendham, near Saxmundham, Suffolk, in 1907. Loaned to the Museum in 1961, it was purchased in 1965 for £15,500, with contributions from the Pilgrim Trust, Mr I.D. Margary, the NACF and All Souls College. H. 30 cm

British Museum Act 1963

CHAPTER 24

ARRANGEMENT OF SECTIONS

Section
1.   Altered composition of British Museum Trustees.
2.   General powers of Trustees.
3.   Keeping and inspection of collections.
4.   Lending of objects.
5.   Disposal of objects.
6.   Staff.
7.   Reports by Trustees.
8.   Separation of Natural History Museum.
9.   Transfers to other institutions.
10. Authorised repositories.
11. Amendment of 57 & 58 Vict. c. 34.
12. Expenses of additional repositories and storage premises.
13. Short title, commencement, transitional provisions and repeals.

SCHEDULES:
First Schedule—Tenure of office and proceedings of Trustees.
Second Schedule—Transitional provisions as to separation of Natural History Museum.
Third Schedule—Sites of authorised repositories.
Fourth Schedule—Repeals.

2 Above: The British Museum Act (1963) which superseded that of 1753. The new Act maintained the Museum's link with Parliament which had established it. *Ex officio* and family Trustees were removed and the Board reduced to twenty-five. The independence of the Natural History Museum was recognised and loans from the collections made easier.

3 Right: The proposed new buildings to the south of the Museum, designed by Leslie Martin and Colin St John Wilson (1962), were intended to provide space for the library and new facilities for public and staff. While St George's Church and the Pharmaceutical Society would have been preserved, the new building would have replaced the existing streets and alleyways and was therefore opposed by the local authority. The King's Library and round Reading Room would most probably have remained in library use.

4 Left: Roundel from a Roman mosaic floor, 4th century AD, found on the site of a villa at Hinton St Mary, Dorset, in 1963 when post holes were being dug for the foundations of a building in a field near a blacksmith's forge. Purchased from the landowner. It is the earliest known representation of the head of Christ yet found in Britain. L. (of mosaic) 8.1 m

5 Frog made of andesite porphyry, Egypt, c. 3100 BC, offered for purchase in 1966, with other items, through the will of the late Captain Edward G. Spencer Churchill, and bought for £2,000. L. 30.8 cm

6 Paul Gauguin (1848–1903), Two Marquesans. A monotype from the bequest of sixteen important 19th-century French drawings, including works by Degas, Pissarro, Renoir, Seurat and Toulouse Lautrec, made by the French dealer and scholar César Mange de Hauke (1900–65) in appreciation for the help he had received in the Print Room. 32.1 x 50.9 cm

7 Right: Silver gilt cup and cover, and a sideboard dish, by Paul de Lamerie (1687–1751), from a bequest by Peter Wilding (d. 1969) of over forty pieces of silver plate made in London by Huguenot craftsmen 1697–1730, one of the finest privatecollections of such material. H. (of cup) 29.2 cm

8 Right: Korean lacquered wooden box inlaid with mother-of-pearl, tortoise shell and metal wire, made to house Buddhist sutras, Koryo dynasty, 13th century AD. Bought for £6,000 in 1966 with the aid of the Brooke Sewell bequest. One of only eight such boxes known. L. 47.2 cm

9 Left: The Dunstable swan jewel, a livery badge made in France or England c. 1400, was found during excavations at a Dominican Priory in Dunstable, Bedfordshire, in 1965. Bought in 1966 for £5,000 with the aid of the NACF, the Pilgrim Trust, the Worshipful Company of Goldsmiths, it is the sole surviving example of such a badge. H. 3.3 cm

'The Tutankhamun exhibition at the British Museum was seen by 4,400 people on Thursday, when it opened to the public. When the first ticket was sold in the morning to a man who had queued for 14 hours, 1,500 people were behind him. By midday the queue had grown to 2,500 and stretched 300 yards…

From today those in the queue will be able to use a special "restaurant" built during the last week in the forecourt of the Museum and designed to serve 600 visitors an hour… On Monday the exhibition will open between 10 am and 2 pm for school parties only. Although schoolchildren are on holiday, 2,000 are expected that day and about 2,400 on subsequent Monday mornings. There are 1,400 schools on the waiting list.'
The Times, *2 April 1972*

1 An exhibition of treasures from the tomb of the Egyptian pharaoh Tutankhamun, loaned by the Cairo Museum and sponsored jointly by the British Museum, *The Times* and *The Sunday Times*, was held from 30 March to 31 December 1972. It was seen by 1,669,117 visitors.

2 Above: In 1778 Captain Cook's expedition visited Vancouver Island. This alderwood bowl, carved by a Mowachaht artist, was probably acquired then. Bought by the Museum in 1971, it was at one time in the collection of Sir Ashton Lever whose museum, the Holophusicon, opened in Leicester Square in February 1775. Lever's collection was disposed of by lottery and later dispersed. The sculptor Henry Moore's (p. 54) depiction of women and children was influenced by these figures. *L. 20 cm*

3 Head of an unnamed Egyptian official, *c.* 665 BC, excavated at the temple of Mut, Karnak, by Margaret Benson and Janet Gourlay in 1895. Their foreman received 10d a day instead of the normal 7½d to compensate him for loss of prestige working under female supervision. Bought in 1973 with the aid of the NACF. *H. 19.5 cm*

5 Right: Selection from a find of around 55,000 coins, *c.* AD 200–270, from Mildenhall, Wiltshire. Known as the 'Cunetio hoard' after the Roman name for the town and to distinguish it from Mildenhall, Suffolk. Found in 1978 buried in a storage jar and lead container, it is the largest hoard of Roman coins so far discovered in Britain.

4 Right: *Night on the El Train*, print by the American artist Edward Hopper (1882–1967), 1918, from the collection given by Campbell Dodgson (p. 47) in 1926. From the late 1970s the Museum embarked on a major expansion of its 20th-century collections. This print was in 1980 included in an exhibition, 'American prints 1879–1979'. The new range extended to Canadian, Latin American, German, French, Scandinavian, Israeli and British holdings. In addition to prints and drawings the Museum began to focus on other 'modern' areas. *18.3 x 20.1 cm*

6 Left: Francisco Goya (1746–1828), *Self-portrait*, 1799, the first plate from the etching series *Los Caprichos*, a series of 80 satirical prints. With the acquisition in 1975 of the collection of 2,400 Goya prints made by Tomás Harris (d. 1963), accepted in lieu of estate duty, the Museum now possesses the largest collection of Goya prints in the world. *21.7 x 15.1 cm*

7 Chinese bronze ritual vessel, 11th century BC, known as the *Kang Hou gui*. It is famous for its inscription describing an attack on the Shang by the Zhou king and the establishment of the Kang Hou (Marquis of Kang). Acquired in 1977 with the aid of the Brooke Sewell Fund and Bequest, and the Planelles-Granell Bequest. *H. 21.6 cm*

8 Above: Museum Street by Andrew Murray. With the implementation of the British Library Act (1972) in July 1973, the Museum's library departments joined with other libraries to form a new institution. The decision to move the library to a new site at St Pancras was taken in 1976. The Ethnographic collections were 'temporarily' transferred to the Museum of Mankind which opened at Burlington Gardens in 1970 and has since closed in preparation for the return of Ethnography to Bloomsbury.

9 Votive plaque from the earliest hoard of Christian liturgical silver yet found in the Roman Empire, 4th century AD. The twenty-eight pieces, acquired as treasure trove, were discovered in 1975 by a man walking across a recently ploughed field at Water Newton (*Durobrivae*), Cambridgeshire, looking for clay pipes and pottery. *H. 15.7 cm*

10 Porcelain *meiping* (prunus blossom bottle), Ming dynasty, early 15th century AD, made in Jingdezhen, China, given by US Ambassador Walter Annenberg in 1972. In 1996 Ambassador and Mrs Annenberg were to provide £6 million to fund the refurbishment and redevelopment of the Reading Room. *H. 33.2 cm*

"There is a Supreme God in the Ethnological Section," wrote William Empson, the best single line ever written about the Museum. For not only are the treasures of the past here, its terrors and small household implements, but its gods are here as well.

As you walk through the galleries you begin to feel like a god yourself. As gallery follows gallery you see the nations stir, stumble upright, stamp out of some small land to bring devastation, and then fall back. Another gallery, and their conquerors begin the same cycle...

There is so much to see that you become a jaded time-traveller remembering only the spectacular: Tiglath-Pileser, a curled Assyrian bull, counting his heaps of severed heads; an arm bigger than the body of a man in the Egyptian galleries, and your senses reel at what this was once joined to among the sands... Then you turn a corner, and the light is dazzling. You are in the Classical world of beauty and air. It is the most extraordinary experience as the catalogue of death gives way to a celebration of youth.'

Byron Rogers, 'All ye need to know on earth', Observer, 5 April 1981

1 Henry Moore (1898–1986), *Crowd looking at a tied-up object*, 1942. Based on a photograph of West African masquerade. One of nine drawings from the estate of Lord Clark of Saltwood, allocated to the Museum in 1988 in lieu of Capital Transfer Tax. With existing holdings, these make the Museum's collection of Moore drawings the most numerous outside the Henry Moore Foundation. *44.2 x 57.1 cm*

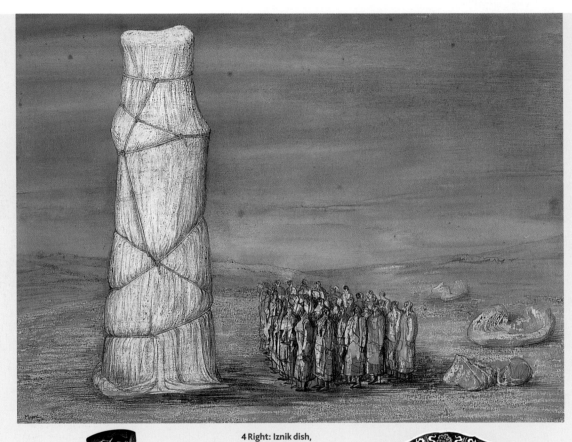

2 Below: Figure from a ritual house of the Wosera Abelam of East Sepik Province, Papua New Guinea, part of a collection of 474 carvings and paintings on bark purchased from the villagers in 1980. Collecting expeditions to the region were also mounted in 1963–4 and the 1980s. *H. 2.2 m (approx.)*

4 Right: Iznik dish, Ottoman Turkey, *c.* 1550–70. Frederick Ducane Godman (1834–1919) built up a collection of some 600 Islamic ceramics. Its acquisition (part bequest, part in lieu of capital transfer tax), after the death of his daughter Edith in 1982, gave the Museum the best Iznik collection in the world. *Diam. 38.8 cm*

3 Gold and cloisonné enamel locket by the Maison Falize, Paris, *c.* 1868–70. One of 1,200 jewels dating largely from the 17th to mid-20th century AD given by Professor and Mrs Anne Hull Grundy in 1978. Their gifts and final bequest in 1984 also included 1,000 Japanese netsuke and inro. *H. 5.4 cm*

5 Left: 2 lira note of the Banco di Sicilia, 1866. In a single decade the Museum's collection of paper money grew from a modest and randomly acquired assortment to a position of international eminence. Over 9,000 notes from the collection of the Marquis of Bute were acquired in 1984. *14.2 x 20.6 cm*

6 Fragments of wooden writing tablets dating from c. AD 97–103 were found between 1973 and 1997 at excavations directed by Robin Birley at the Roman fort of Vindolanda (modern Chesterholm), Northumberland, close to Hadrian's Wall. This tablet is an invitation to a birthday party. *L. 22.3 cm*

7 'Collector' with female portraits strung around his neck (1985). Medal by the Polish medallist Piotr Gowron (b. 1943), cast bronze, partly enamelled. An example of the modern medals acquired in recent years. The Museum has a total collection of some 70,000 medals. *13.2 x 10.5 cm*

8 Above: The Portland Vase was smashed into about 200 pieces in 1845 but reassembled by the Museum's restorer John Doubleday. After its purchase in 1945 it was taken apart and repaired. In 1988 the vase was again restored by Museum conservator Nigel Williams using an epoxy resin.

The conservators and scientists of the Museum bring a wide range of skills to the preservation and investigation of the collections. Although they work largely behind the scenes, the great majority of objects on display have received their attention.

9 Shiva Nataraja (dancing Shiva in a ring of fire), South Indian bronze, c. AD 1100, acquired in 1987. One of many objects bought with a gift and bequest, amounting to over £1 million, given by a merchant banker, P.T. Brooke-Sewell (d. 1958), which continues to enable the Department of Asia to expand its collections. *H. 89.5 cm*

10 Right: Tiffany vase, American, made c. 1896–1928. In 1979 the Museum began to extend its post-medieval collections of ceramics, glass and metalwork into the 20th century. A 20th-century gallery was opened in 1982. *Diam 22.1 cm*

'The British Museum used to be the most serious place in London. The bowed backs of antiquarians would droop like so many flaccid cocktail sausages over the dusty artefacts, and even the tourists wore conscientious expressions... But something is stirring beneath the mummified bandages. Along the way from the Stone Age and Roman Britain rooms, just around the corner from Early and Coptic Egypt, three new galleries have burst out of the unpromising sarcophagus of the jewellery room.

It's a revolution. For the first time, the Museum's 19th Century collections have been given a gallery all to themselves. Most people will be dumbstruck to hear that the British Museum even possesses things that are barely a century or so old. And not everything's made of stone, either. There's glass, ceramics, gold and, tucked away in the tiny 20th Century room, there's even plastic.'

Alice Freeman, 'Keeping the Victorians amused', Daily Express, *3 September 1994*

1 In March 1998, with the removal of the British Library to St Pancras, work began on the construction of the Queen Elizabeth II Great Court. The roof is made of 3,312 unique triangular glazed panels attached to a steel structure. The cost of the project was £110 million. Among the major donors were the Weston family, the Millennium Commission and the Heritage Lottery Fund.

2 Above: The 5th-century AD treasure from Hoxne, Suffolk, was discovered in 1992 by a man searching with a metal detector for a friend's lost hammer, and comprises 15,000 coins and about 200 gold and silver objects, including 98 spoons and ladles. The hoard was immediately reported by its finder, so it could be professionally excavated. Judged to be treasure trove, a full reward of £1.75 million was paid. The treasure was acquired with the assistance of the NHMF, NACF, Lloyds Private Banking, the BMF, and generous private donations. The Weston Gallery of Roman Britain, opened 1997, revealed the richness of what was at one time considered an unimportant part of the Empire.

3 Uncovering the remains of the Early Bronze Age Palace destroyed by fire c. 2700 BC at Tell es-Sa'idiyeh, Jordan, in an excavation conducted between 1985 and 1996 by Jonathan Tubb of the Department of the Ancient Near East. Museum staff continue to excavate at home and abroad.

4 Right: Known as the 'Warren cup' after Edward Perry Warren, an art-lover and collector who acquired it a century ago, this unique Roman silver drinking cup, made mid-1st century AD, was bought for £1.8 million with the assistance of the HLF, NACF, BMF, the Caryatid Fund, Mr Claude Hankes-Drielsma, Dr Roy Lennox and Ms Joan Weberman, and Mr and Mrs Richard Kan. It is said to be from Bittir (ancient Bethther), near Jerusalem. *H. 11 cm*

5 Left: The Corbridge lanx (tray), 4th century AD, part of a hoard of late Roman silver discovered in 1735 on the banks of the River Tyne, Northumberland, by a nine-year-old girl, Isabel Cutter. Other Roman vessels were recovered in the vicinity between 1731 and 1760, but only this survived. Previously owned by the Duke of Northumberland, in 1993 it was acquired from the government, partly in lieu of taxes and also with the aid of grants from the NHMF, NACF and the BMF. *L. 50.6 cm*

6 Below: White porcelain 'moon jar', Choson dynasty, 17th to 18th century AD, acquired with the assistance of the Hahn Kwang-Ho Purchase Fund for Korean Art. The jar was in 1935 bought in an antique shop in Seoul by the noted potter Bernard Leach (1887–1979) and later given by him to the potter Lucie Rie (1902–95). On her death she bequeathed it to Janet Leach from whose estate it was purchased in 1999. From its late 19th-century beginnings, the Korean collection expanded greatly during the 1980s and 1990s. The Korea Foundation Gallery opened in 2000. *H. 47 cm*

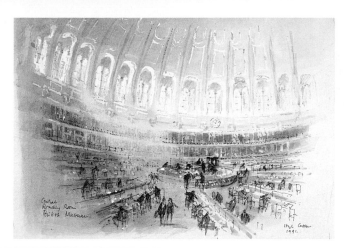

7 Drawing of the round Reading Room in 1991 by Sir Hugh Casson (1910–99). The Reading Room was closed to readers on 27 October 1997 as the British Library transferred its collections to the new building at St Pancras. *32 x 46 cm*

8 Above: A collection of over 1 million cigarette and trade cards, given by Edward Wharton Tigar (1913–95). Following a colourful life as a mining engineer, he wrote in his biography 'If to collect cigarette cards is a sign of eccentricity, how then will posterity judge one who amassed the biggest collection in the world? Frankly, I care not'. The collection is the finest in the world – of interest in the history of printing, advertising, trade and popular culture.

9 Left: Items from a hoard of about fifty broken torcs, seventy bracelets and other items, found in 1990 and acquired by the Museum as treasure trove. Since 1948 at least eleven hoards of coins, torcs, bracelets, ingots and scrap (around 20 kg of silver and 15 kg of gold), most buried *c.* 70 BC, have been found at Ken Hill, Snettisham, East Anglia.

10 Tibetan ceremonial conch shell trumpet, mounted in gilded copper, probably 18th century. Acquired in 1992 as part of a collection of 114 Japanese tea wares and 132 items of Tibetan art, built up between the 1940s and 1970s by the collectors Johannes Schmitt and Mareta Meade. Given through the BMF. *H. 44 cm*

'When the British Museum's Queen Elizabeth II Great Court opens next week, you will see a quite extraordinary transformation. Millions of visitors – because the museum is immensely popular and free of charge – will wander casually through the new South Portico into the luminous expanse of the Great Court. There they will be rooted to the spot. Gazing upwards, transfixed in awe. The best architecture has always played this game of sudden revelation.

And Lord Foster, architect of the £100m project, is a master of the game. Although from the outside – such is the British way – you scarcely know anything has happened behind its august Ionic portico, the nation's prime cultural repository is no longer a collection of awkwardly connected, mid-19th-century galleries.'
Hugh Pearman, 'The Court of Appeal', Sunday Times Magazine, *26 November 2000*

1 The Queen Elizabeth II Great Court, a name which echoes the 'great court' at the front of 17th-century Montagu House (p. 8). The new building, designed by Lord Foster of Thames Bank, OM, was opened by the Queen on 6 December 2000.

2 Above: Commemorative medal specially produced by the Royal Mint to mark the 250th anniversary of the foundation of the Museum in 2003. Designed by John Maine, RA, the square, the circle and the triangle suggest the simple geometry underpinning the culturally diverse objects within the Museum's collections. On one side the implied cubic form encircled by the border of the medal evokes an object within the Museum's care. *Diam. 38.61 mm*

3 View of the roof of the Queen Elizabeth II Great Court at night from Centre Point. This is now a major new landmark visible from the 'London Eye'.

4 Right: The restored decoration of the Reading Room (detail), as it would have been seen by Karl Marx and others shortly after the opening in 1857.

5 Sherds of Middle Neolithic pottery, approx. 8,000 years old. From a collection of about 6 million ancient Egyptian and Sudanese artefacts acquired by Professor Fred Wendorf, of the Department of Anthropology, Southern Methodist University of Dallas, Texas, from excavations carried out between 1963 and 1977, and given to the Museum in 2002. The collection, which ranges in age from half a million to 5,000 years old, includes a 13,000-year-old burial site believed to contain the oldest evidence of organised warfare. The collection is of major importance to scholarship, extending the Museum's archaeological reach both geographically and chronologically.

6 Below: 'A fine dog it was, and a lucky dog was I to purchase it' wrote Henry Jennings (1731–1819). He acquired the nickname of 'Dog-Jennings' having in 1753–6 bought from Bartolomeo Cavaceppi this Roman marble copy of a lost Greek original of the 2nd century BC, portraying a hound from Molossia (north-west Greece/Albania). Plagued by debts, Jennings in 1816 sold the dog to T. Duncombe, MP. It remained in Duncombe Park until 1983. Acquired for £679,297.82 in 2001 with the assistance of the HLF, NACF, Duthie Fund, BMF, Ready Bequest, the Caryatid Fund, Mrs Barbara G. Fleischman, Mr and Mrs Frank A. Ladd, and a public appeal. H. 1.05 m (max.)

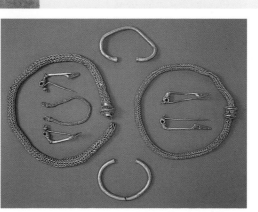

7 The 'Braganza brooch', probably made by a Greek or Greek-trained craftsman in the Iberian peninsula, c. 250–200 BC, for a Celtic prince. Collected by HRH Ferdinand of Saxe-Coburg. From 1919 to 1941 owned by HRH Nevada (1885–1941) of the Portugese royal house of Braganza, and later by Thomas Flannery Jnr. It was bought in 2001 with the help of the HLF, NACF, Duthie Fund, Roy Lennox and Joan Weberman and the BMF. L. 14 cm (max.)

8 Right: Float from the Japanese Nebuta festival, illuminated by over 800 light bulbs, constructed at the Museum as part of Japan 2001 by Takashi Kitamura in partnership with Aomori City and with the support of The Daiwa Anglo-Japanese Foundation. Made of wood, wire and painted paper, Nebuta are gigantic lanterns – up to 5 metres high and 9 metres wide – which depict dramatic three-dimensional scenes drawn from Japanese history, legend or folklore.

9 Right: The Winchester hoard, Iron Age, c. 75–25 BC, found in 2000 by metal detector in a field near Winchester, the most important discovery of Iron Age gold objects from Britain since 1950. Made of 1,160 grams of a very pure gold, the hoard comprises two sets of gold jewellery, each with a necklace, torc and two gold brooches held together by a chain. There are also two gold bracelets. As it was promptly reported, archaeologists were able to investigate the field to find out more about the hoard's context. Bought with the help of the NHMF, the NACF and the BMF.

BM Friends

The Friends of the British Museum are now an essential source of funds for acquisitions for the Museum's collections and, interestingly, this is why an earlier group of supporters was established in 1901 when a number of 'anonymous gentlemen', led by Max Rosenheim, banded together to buy objects to fill the gap left by the death of Sir Augustus Wollaston Franks in 1897 (p. 29). The Friends of the British Museum merged with the infant National Art Collections Fund in 1904, which has since been a major and continuing contributor to the Museum's collections.

The Friends were re-established in 1968. Since 1974, having returned their start-up costs to the Museum, they have donated or contributed to the acquisition of hundreds of individual objects and collections. A selection is shown here.

The Friends also support excavations, exhibitions and other activities such as educational programmes. Their volunteers assist in a wide range of projects throughout the Museum. The total of the Friends' donations and grants exceeds £2.5 million.

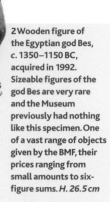

2 Wooden figure of the Egyptian god Bes, c. 1350–1150 BC, acquired in 1992. Sizeable figures of the god Bes are very rare and the Museum previously had nothing like this specimen. One of a vast range of objects given by the BMF, their prices ranging from small amounts to six-figure sums. *H. 26.5 cm*

1 Pablo Picasso (1881–1973), *Large dancing nude*, 1962. The acquisition of this linocut in 1999, with a contribution from the BMF, continued the Department of Prints & Drawings' policy of adding key prints by Picasso to the Museum's collection. From 1983 the BMF has granted an annual sum of money to buy contemporary works of art on paper, the first of a number of similar 'running' funds to collect modern material such as board games, eastern European and Central Asian textiles, and contemporary medals. *64 x 53 cm*

3 Right: Festive costume from the Mariovo district, FYR Macedonia. Collected by Dr Diane Waller in the 1960s. Bought with the assistance of the BMF (Eastern European Purchase Fund, established in 1993 and expanded in 1997 to include Central Asia). The Museum now has one of the finest collections of Balkan costume in the world. The BMF have also supported fieldwork in areas such as Madagascar and Papua New Guinea.

4 Burse (purse) made to hold the Great Seal of Queen Elizabeth I, carried in procession before the Lord Chancellor and Keeper of the Seal. The Keeper, Sir Thomas Egerton, gave the burse to his servant Henry Jones, whose family transformed it into a cushion cover. Acquired with the aid of the NHMF, NACF and BMF. *H. 43 cm*

5 Right: Inscribed bowl of Artaxerxes I (r. 464–424 BC), Achaemenid. One of a group of four similar examples which were found some time before 1935. Previously the Museum had no example of Persian gold or silver plate with a royal inscription. Bought with the help of the BMF, NACF and Friends of the Ancient Near East. *Diam. 29 cm*

6 Below: Wooden coffin and lid of the Lady of the House Nesmut, *c.* 720 BC, from Thebes, Egypt. Among a group presented by the Egyptian government to the Prince of Wales in 1869. The coffin and lid were then given to the 3rd Duke of Sutherland, one of the Prince's travelling companions, and exhibited in the museum at Dunrobin Castle, Sutherland, Scotland. Bought with the aid of the BMF in 2000. *L. (of lid) 1.85 m*

7 Left: Nasca (AD 1–700) vessel showing an agricultural deity. The BMF's Townley Group supports key projects, among them the production of an archive of Nasca designs, funding excavations at Knidos (p. 25), the study of the archives of Charles Masson (p. 39), recording the Mildenhall Treasure site (p. 46), conserving architectural plans, and conserving human remains in the Wendorf collection. (p. 58). *H. 16.5 cm*

8 Max Rosenheim (d. 1911), founder of the first Friends of the British Museum, a major collector and generous donor of a wide range of objects including medals and 10,000 bookplates.

9 Below: Solid silver tigress inlaid in niello from the Hoxne hoard (p. 56), Roman Britain, buried in the 5th century AD. The BMF has assisted in the purchase of material from several hoards, among them the Corbridge lanx (p. 56), Milton Keynes, Oxfordshire, Alton (Hants), Salcombe Bay, Fincham and Appledore. *L. 15.9 cm*

10 Above: Terracotta group of three female dancers in a ring, Mycenaean, *c.* 1300 BC, from the Hirsch and Virsi collections. Purchased with the help of the BMF. *H. 6.5 cm*

11 Right: Lacquered and gilded Chinese Buddha, 15th century AD, Ming dynasty. Given by the BMF in 1985. *H. 43.8 cm*

12 Right: Indian Monopoly. Part of an expanding worldwide collection of board games funded by the BMF, which includes Indian pachisi sets, Javanese mancala gaming boards, a Korean Nyout set, an English Braille chess set and modern Syrian games.

Major Benefactors of the British Museum

1700 Sir John Cotton
1743 Arthur Edwards
1753 Sir Hans Sloane
1753 Henrietta, Countess of Oxford
    Margaret, Duchess of Portland
1757 HM King George II
1759 Solomon da Costa
1760 The Earl of Exeter
1766 Gustavus Brander
1769 William Fawkener
1775 Captain James Cook
1779 David Garrick
1798 The Society of Dilettanti
1799 Clayton Mordaunt Cracherode
1799 Sir William Musgrave
1802 HM King George III
1817 The Earl of Aberdeen
1817 Jean Louis Burckhardt
    Henry Salt
1818 Sarah Sophia Banks
    Lady Banks
1820 Sir Joseph Banks
1823 HM King George IV
1823 William White
1824 Richard Payne Knight
1825 Sir Gore Ouseley
1829 The Earl of Bridgewater
1830 Sir Robert Brownrigg
1831 Viscount Kingsborough
1834 William Marsden
1835 Thomas Hardwicke
1835 Lord Prudhoe
1846 Sir Stratford Canning
1846 Thomas Grenville
1851 Sir Austen Henry Layard
1851 William Smith
1852 Henry Crowe
    Thomas B. Murray
1854 Assyrian Excavation Fund
1855 Chambers Hall
1856 Sir William Temple
1858 Brian Houghton Hodgson
1859 John Francis William de Salis
1859 Sir Thomas Stamford Raffles
    W.C. Raffles Flint
1861 The Earl of Aberdeen
1864 Edward Wigan
1865 Henry Christy
1866 James Woodhouse
1868 Felix Slade
1868 Chauncey Hare Townshend
1869 HM Queen Victoria
1872 Mrs John Bridge
    Fanny Bridge
    Mrs Edgar Barker
1874 Sir Charles Fellows, Lady Fellows
1877 The Governor and Company
    of the Bank of England
1878 John Henderson
1878 Augustus Meyrick
1880 The India Office
1880 John Jope Rogers
1882 Isabella Bewick
1882 Sir Flinders Petrie
1883 The Egypt Exploration Society
1883 Charles Whately
1885 Sir Ernest Satow
1886 The Earl of Chichester
1888 Octavius Morgan
1889 Sir Harold Deane
1891 Mrs J.W. Cross ('George Eliot')
    Mrs Gertrude Lewes
1891 Mrs Eliza Cruikshank
1891 Thomas Keay Tapling
1894 Sir Alexander Cunningham
    Allan J.C. Cunningham
1894 William Greenwell
1895 William Gibbs
1895 John Malcolm of Poltalloch
    Lord Malcolm of Poltalloch
1895 William Mitchell
1895 Lady Charlotte Schreiber

1896 Lady Llanover
1897 Sir Augustus Wollaston Franks
1898 Baron Ferdinand Rothschild
1899 Charles Drury Edward Fortnum
1899 Vincent Stuckey Lean
1899 Henry Vaughan
1900 Henry Spencer Ashbee
1902 Lord Cheylesmore
1903 HM King Edward VII
1904 National Art Collections Fund
1906 Frederick Parkes Weber
1908 Sir Thomas Brooke
1908 J. Pierpont Morgan
1909 Isaac Falcke
1909 George Salting
1910 Alfred Henry Huth
1911 British School of Archaeology in Egypt
1912 Lady Layard
1913 Arthur Henry Sanxay Barwell
1913 The Earl of Crawford and Balcarres
1913 Sir William Gwynne-Evans
1916 P. Amaury Talbot
1917 Baroness Lucas and Dingwall
1917 George Peel
1917 Baroness Zouche of Haryngworth
1919 Sir John Evans
    Sir Arthur Evans
1919 Henry Yates Thompson
1920 The Worshipful Company of Goldsmiths
1921 Mr and Mrs Frank Lloyd
1922 Contemporary Art Society
1923 Charles Borradaile
1927 George Eumorfopoulos
1929 Guy Brunton
1930 Viscount Gladstone
    H.N. Gladstone
1931 Lord Duveen
1933 George Smith
    Mrs Elizabeth Smith
1934 Thomas Bryan Clarke-Thornhill
1934 The Pilgrim Trust
1935 Thomas George Barnett
1935 Viscountess Gladstone
1937 Charles Ricketts
    Charles Shannon
1938 Thomas William Francis Gann
1938 Sir Robert Mond
1938 May Morris
1939 Mrs Rudyard Kipling
1939 Mrs Edith May Pretty
1940 Charles Gabriel Seligman
    Mrs Brenda Z. Seligman
1941 Oscard Charles Raphael
1941 Mrs Henry Yates Thompson
1944 Harry G. Beasley
    Mrs H.G. Beasley
1945 Matilda Theresa Talbot
1946 HM King George VI
1946 Joseph John Acworth
    Mrs Marion Whiteford Acworth
1946 Gertrude Mary Coles
    Percival Chater Manuk
1946 Albert Hugh Lloyd
    Muriel Eleanor Haydon Lloyd
    Mrs A.H. Lloyd
1946 Harry James Oppenheim
1946 Count Antoine Seilern
1948 Campbell Dodgson
1948 Sir Bernard Eckstein
1950 George Bernard Shaw
1954 The Wellcome Trust
1955 Sir Chester Beatty
1956 Sir Alan Gardiner
1956 Webster Plass
    Mrs Webster Plass
1957 HM Queen Elizabeth II
1958 Gilbert Harold Samuel Edgard
1958 Robert Wylie Lloyd
1958 C.F.I. Ramsden
1958 Percy Thomas Brooke Sewell
1959 Sir Ambrose Heal
1960 Ursula Vaughan Williams

1961 Dame Joan Evans
1963 Alfred Walter Francis Fuller
    Estelle Winifred Fuller
1965 César Mange de Hauke
1966 Eric George Millar
1967 Mr and Mrs Albert Ehrman
1967 Mrs Walter Sedgwick
1968 Mrs Olga A. Hirsch
1969 John Roland Abbey
1969 Peter Wilding
1974 The British Museum Friends
1974 Sir Harry and Lady Garner
1974 Henry Moore
1975 Tomás Harris
1976 Royal Anthropological Institute
    of Great Britain and Ireland
1977 Lady Clark
1977 Henry Davis
1978 Patrick Joseph Donnelly
1978 John and Anne Hull Grundy
1981 Collingwood Ingram
1981 National Heritage Memorial Fund
1983 Sir John Addis
1983 Lord Clark
1983 Edith Godman
1987 Richard Boys Lewis
    Mrs G.E.M. Lewis
1990 Asahi Shimbun
1990 Sir Joseph Hotung
1991 Raymond and Beverly Sackler
1991 Lord Wolfson of Marylebone
    The Wolfson Foundation and
    Family Charitable Trust
1992 Korea Foundation
1992 Johannes Schmitt
    Mareta Meade
1993 Consejo Nacional para la
    Cultura y las Artes (Mexico)
1993 Mrs Rosi Schilling
1994 The Chase Manhattan Bank
1995 The British Museum Company Limited
1995 HSBC Holdings Plc
1995 Edward Wharton-Tigar
1996 Annenberg Foundation
    The Honorable and Mrs Walter H. Annenberg
1996 The Clothworkers' Foundation
1996 Mr and Mrs Lawrence A. Fleischman
1996 Mr and Mrs Donald Kahn
1996 The Millennium Commission
1996 The Monument Trust
1996 Sir Robert and Lady Sainsbury
    David Sainsbury
    Susie Sainsbury
1996 The Garfield Weston Foundation
1997 Lord Hamlyn and the Paul Hamlyn Foundation
1997 Heritage Lottery Fund
1997 Hugh and Catherine Stevenson
1998 Hahn Kwang-Ho
1998 Peter Moores
1999 American Friends of the British Museum
1999 The Bioanthropology Foundation
1999 BP Plc
1999 The Clore Foundation and
    the Vivien Duffield Foundation
1999 Mary, Viscountess Eccles
1999 The Kresge Foundation
1999 The Wellcome Trust
2000 The Henry Moore Foundation
2001 Anonymous
2001 The Deborah Loeb Brice Foundation
2001 Sir Harry and Lady Djanogly
2001 Charles A. Hersh
2001 Simon Sainsbury
2002 Professor Fred Wendorf

Illustration References

(including locations of objects currently on display)

Foundation
1 Engraving by John Faber jun., after a painting by Thomas Murray, 1728; PD C.S. 329,I
2 CA; Illustrations of the BM, vol. I, f. 2
3 The Natural History Museum
4 Ethno Sloane 1368. *Room 26*
5 Oil painting by Sir Godfrey Kneller, given by the Duchess of Portland 1768. On loan from the Museum to the British Library
6 Oil painting by Michael Dahl given by the Duchess of Portland 1768. On loan from the Museum to the British Library
7 British Library, Harley MS 4866, f. 88
8 PD Sloane 5218-161
9 P&E Sloane 54; Gunter 290. *Room 42*
10 British Library, Cotton MS Nero D. iv, f. 138v
11 P&E Sloane 246
12 BM; oil painting attr. Cornelis Jonson, 1629
1750s
1 Engraving by Sutton Nicholls, 1714. CA; Illustrations of the BM, vol. I, f. 10
2 Coloured engraving. Mummy: AES 6695
3 CA; Illustrations of the BM, vol. II, f. 33
4 British Library Royal MS. 2B. vii, f. 151
5 The Natural History Museum, presented by George Edwards
1760s
1 GR 1760.9-19.1; Bronze 847. *Room 22*
2 PD 1983 u 2965
3 CL
4 P&E 1763,4-15,1 & 2; Porcelain Cat II 28. *Room 46*
1770s
1 National Portrait Gallery
2 Ethno Tah 78
3 GR 1772.3-20.30; Vase E 224. *Room 19*
4 CA; Illustrations of the BM, vol. I, f. 125
5 BM; oil painting, anon. artist
6 CL; J. and A. van Rymsdyk
7 P&E 1887,3-7.I.70; Pottery Cat. I.70. *Room 46*
8 Ethno NZ 113
9 J.B. Smith after Benjamin West; PD 1841-8-9-150
10 CL; J. and A. van Rymsdyk
1780s
1 PD 1862-6-14-631
2 PD 1998-4-25-5
3 P&E 1786,5-27.1; Pottery Cat. I.712. *Room 47*
4 Watercolour by Samuel Hieronymus Grimm, purchased in 1984; PD 1984-5-12-4
1790s
1 PD Gg.2-259
2 Engraving by W.H. Worthington after Henry Eldridge; *Biographical Decameron*, 1817; PD 1853-12-10-636
3 CM BMC 7
4 CA
5 PD 1928-7-14-2
1800s
1 Aquatint by A.C. Pugin and T. Rowlandson, published by R. Ackermann in *The Microcosm of London* (1808–11). CA; Illustrations of the BM, vol. I, f. 20, pl. 14
2 AES 24. *Room 4*
3 GR 1805.7-3.79; Sculpture 1874. *Room 84*
4 Drawing by C. John M. Whichelo, 1812, purchased 1958; PD 1958-10-11-8
5 Johann Zoffany (1733–1810). Burnley Museums and Art Galleries. Townley Hall Gallery
6 From the *Déscription de l'Égypt* (1809–28), vol. V. Fist: AES 9. *Room 4*
7 GR 1805.7-3.43; Sculpture 250. *Main Staircase*
8 CA; Illustrations of the BM, vol. I, f. 169. Sarcophagus: AES 10. *Room 4*
1810s
1 GR South frieze slab XLIV. *Room 18*
2 BM; oil painting by Archibald Archer, 1819.
3 PD 1881-7-9-346
4 CA; cartoon by George Cruikshank, 1819
5 AES 19. *Room 4*
6 Ethno Library; T.E. Bowdich, 1818
7 Ethno 1818,11-14.23
8 CM Banks NJC 148. *Room 46*
9 *Narrative of the operations and recent discoveries within the pyramids, temples, tombs and excavations in Egypt and Nubia* (1820)

10 Engraving after C.R. Cockerell, one of the excavators. Sculptures: GR 1815.10-20. *Room 16*
11 CA; W.S.W. Vaux, *Handbook to the Antiquities of the British Museum* (1851)
1820s
1 GR 1824.4-27.1; Bronze 1614. *Room 71*
2 PD Pp.3-202
3 Drawing for the *Stationers' Almanack*, 1852, of an impression of Frederick Mackenzie's lithograph of 1844 made for Sir Robert Smirke; PD 1901-5-8-1
4 ANE 89147; 1825,5.3.140
5 OA 1826.2-11.1. *Room 33*
6 PD 2002-2-27-1
7 ANE 118838; 1825,4.21.3. *Room 52*
8 Drawing by George Scharf Snr; PD 1862-6-14-788
1830s
1 CA; *London Interiors*, 1841
2 P&E 1831,11-1.78-159; Iv. Cat. 79. *Room 42*
3 AES 117. *Room 4*
4 OA 1830.6-12.4. *Room 33*
5 OA 1830.6-12.1. *Room 34*
6 CA; *Illustrated London News*, 13 February 1847
7 Ethno 1839,4-26.8
8 AES 15. *Room 4*
9 GR 1836.2-24.127; Cat Vases B. 210. *Room 13*
10 P&E 1836 9-2 1. *Room 36*
1840s
1 Watercolour by J.W. Archer, 1840s; PD 1868-6-12-1799
2 GR 1848.10-20.1; Sculpture B 287. *Room 15*
3 P&E 1847 2-8 82. *Room 50*
4 GR Archive
5 PD 1862-6-14-1061
6 Ethno 1849,6-29.8. *Room 27*
7 PD 1891-11-17-561
8 P&E 1841,7-11,1-741; CM 1838.7-10; *Room 41*
9 PD 1902-1-29-1
10 Drawing from A.H. Layard, *Nineveh and its Remains* (1851), p. 225. Obelisk: ANE 118885; 1848,11.4.1. *Room 6*
1850s
1 Contemporary print of the Reading Room, published in the *Illustrated London News*, 9 May 1857, to mark its opening. CA; Illustrations of the BM, vol. II, f. 38
2 PD
3 P&E 1855,12-1.5. *Room 42*
4 P&E 1857 7-15 1. *Room 50*
5 PD 1983 u 2962
6 PD 1857-7-11-77
7 ANE original drawings, vol. IV, misc 7
8 GR Archive; Lion: GR 1859.12-26.24; Sculpture 1350. *Great Court*
9 Ethno 1859,12-28.201
10 GR 1859.12-26.26; Sculpture 1300. *Room 22*
11 ANE 124875; 1856,9.9.48. *Room 10*
12 CA; *Illustrated London News*, 28 February 1852
13 GR 1857.12-20.232; Sculpture 1000. *Room 21*
14 P&E 1855,12-1.96. *Room 46*
15 CA; Illustrations of the BM, vol. II, f. 42
1860s
1 Ethno Library. Statue: Ethno 1869,10-5.1. *Wellcome Gallery*
2 GR 1867.5-7.484; Gems 3577. *Room 70*
3 OA 1866.12-29.61. *Room 34*
4 CM M.6903; Edward Hawkins Collection. *Room 46*
5 P&E Archive
6 Ethno 1894-634. *Room 27*
7 Getty Images
8 OA 1869.1-20.3. *Room 34*
9 Smith and Porcher, *History of the Recent Discoveries at Cyrene* (1864), pl. 9
10 GR 1861.7-25.1; Sculpture 1380. *Room 22*
11 CM Portraits of Numismatists, vol i
12 P&E 1867,1-20.1. *Room 41*
1870s
1 CA; photograph by Frederick York
2 Ethno 1878,11-1.48
3 ANE K.3375. *Room 55*
4 CA; *Illustrated London News*, 26 September 1874
5 OA 1878.12-30.682. *Room 34*
6 OA 1872.7-1.60. *Room 33*
7 AES 9999/43; 1872,11.1.1
8 GR Ephesus Misc photos, vol. II, p. 12, xxviii B (65)
9 GR 1872.8-3.9; Sculpture 1206. *Room 22*

1880s
1 P&E Sieveking Cat. 555. *Room 36*
2 JA JP 1375; 1881.12-10.1710
3 JA F 1021
4 P&E 1888,12-1.100. *Room 44*
5 PD 1921-10-18-1
6 CL; Felix Leigh, *London Town* (verses), illus. Thomas Crane and Ellen Houghton (1883)
7 British Library; *Comic News*, 18 July 1863
8 AES 21810; 1888,8.6.8. *Room 62*
9 OA 1880.7-9.79. *Room 33a*
10 P&E 1883,12-14,13-16. *Room 41*
11 P&E Archive
1890s
1 CA; *Illustrated London News*, 8 February 1890
2 GR 1897.4-1.1150; Vase C 416. *Room 12*
3 P&E WB 67. *Room 45*
4 PD Schreiber 29
5 CL; M.J. Guest (ed.), *Lady Charlotte Schreiber's Journals*, 2 vols (1911)
6 CM 1894.5-6.962. *Room 68*
7 PD 1895-9-15-474
8 Ethno 1898,9-8.10a. *Room 26*
9 P&E 1893 12-28 15-17. *Room 36*
10 Ethno 1898-1
11 ANE 124017 (OT 116); 1897,12.31.116. *Room 52*
12 PD 1897-5-5-746
13 P&E 1892,5-1.1. *Room 42*
14 Ethno 1898,1-15.30
1900s
1 AES 32751; 1900,10.18.1. *Room 64*
2 P&E 1905,4-18.2
3 CA; courtesy of Mrs M. Pinder
4 CA
5 Ethno Add. MS 39671. *Room 27 (facsimile)*
6 OA 1919.1-1.014
7 AES 684, 685, 686. *Room 4*
8 CM Archive; November 1913
9 Purchased from Captain Johnson in 1903; OA 1903.4-8.1
10 OA 1900.2-9.1. *Room 33*
11 Ethno 1909,12-10.1. *Room 25*
12 CA
1910s
1 PD 1910-2-12-272
2 CM 1911.7-9.2053. *Room 68*
3 CA
4 ANE Archive
5 ANE 118993; 1927,11.14.5. *Room 53*
6 *Daily Sketch*, 8 May 1914
7 OA 1913.11-12.1. *Room 33*
8 GR 1911.9-1.1. *Room 70*
9 JA 1909.6-18.53
10 Ethno LMS.19
1920s
1 PD 1926-10-9-1
2 Ethno Archive; photograph by Henry Sweet
3 Ethno 1886-321
4 Associated Press
5 ANE Archive
6 ANE 122200; 1929,10.17.1. *Room 56*
7 British Film Institute
8 P&E 1924 1-9 1. *Room 50*
9 Ethno 1979.Af1.4546a,b
10 *Punch's Almanac for 1923*, 6 November 1922
1930s
1 Ethno 1939.Af34.1. *Room 25*
2 *Illustrated London News*, 4 December 1937
3 OA 1938.7-15.1. *North Staircase*
4 CA
5 *Evening Standard*, 24 August 1939
6 OA 1936.11-18.1. *Room 33*
7 P&E 1939,10-10.93. *Room 41*
8 P&E Archive
9 AES 64391; 1947,10.11.1. *Room 62*
1940s
1 CA
2 P&E 1946 10-7 1-32. *Room 49*
3 P&E 1967 4-7 1. *Room 49*
4 P&E Eames 4,764-5,421. *Room 43*
5 CA
6 AES Archive
7 Ethno 1947.Af.6.2

8 PD 1949-4-11-80
9 GR 1945.9-27.1; Gems 4036. *Room 70*
10 OA 1948.12-11.025
1950s
1 Chris Ware, Keystone Press Agency, 1954
2 PD 1957-12-14-55
3 P&E 1958,12-2.1. *Room 41*
4 ANE 127412; 1954,5.8.1. *Room 57*
5 *Evening News*, 9 April 1954; PD 1996-7-12-8
6 P&E 1958,10-6.2067
7 P&E Archive
8 Ethno 1954.Af 23.522. *Room 25*
9 GR 1958.4-18.1. *Room 15*
10 ANE 127414; 1954,2.15.1. *Room 59*
1960s
1 P&E 1965 12-1 1. *Room 49*
2 CA
3 CA
4 P&E 1965 4-9 1. *Room 49*
5 AES 66837; 1966,2.12.117. *Room 64*
6 PD 1968-2-10-31
7 P&E 1969,7-5.3 & 25. *Room 46*
8 OA 1966.12-21.1. *Room 67*
9 P&E 1966,7-3.1. *Room 42*
1970s
1 *The Times*
2 Ethno 1971.Am.5.1, NWC 9. *Room 26*
3 AES 67969; 1973,1.20.1
4 PD 1926-6-24-15
5 CM 1983.1-1.3106
6 PD 1975-10-25-420
7 OA 1977.4-4.1. *Room 33*
8 Andrew Murray's London
9 P&E P.1975 10-2 1-28. *Room 49*
10 OA 1972.6-21.1. *Room 33*
1980s
1 PD 1988-3-5-7; reproduced by permission of the Henry Moore Foundation
2 Ethno 1980.Oc11.22
3 P&E Hull Grundy Gift, Cat. 1053
4 OA G.1983.48. *Room 34*
5 CM 1984.6-5.6050
6 P&E 1986 10-1 64. *Room 49*
7 CM 1985.12-35.1
8 BM
9 OA 1987.3-14.1. *Room 33*
10 P&E 1980,11-9.1. *Room 48*
1990s
1 Photo: Phil Sayer
2 P&E P.1994 4-8 1-400. *Room 49*
3 Photo: Alan Hills
4 GR 1999.4-26.1. *Room 70*
5 P&E P.1993 4-1 1. *Room 49*
6 OA 1999.3-2.1. *Room 67*
7 PD 1993-10-2-42; given in 1993 by the Museum's publishing house, British Museum Company Ltd
8 PD
9 P&E 1991 5-1 various. *Room 50*
10 OA 1992.12-14.16. *Room 33*
2000s
1 Photo: Phil Sayer
2 CM
3 Photo: Phil Sayer
4 BM
5 AES
6 GR 2001.10-10.1. *Room 22*
7 GR 2001.5-1.1. *Room 22*
8 Ethno
9 P&E P.2001 9-1 1-10
British Museum Friends
1 PD 1999-9-26-1 © Succession Picasso/DACS 2003
2 AES 74106; 1992,8.19.1. *Room 61*
3 Ethno 1993.Eu7.1-10
4 P&E 1997,3-1.1
5 ANE 1994,1.27.1. *Room 52*
6 AES 75193; 2000,7.24.1. *Room 61*
7 Ethno 1931,11-23.3
8 CM Archive
9 P&E 1994 4-8 30. *Room 49*
10 GR 1996.3-25.1. *Room 12*
11 OA 1985.10-14.1. *Room 33*
12 OA

Acknowledgements

This book is dedicated to all those who have supported the British Museum over the past 250 years and will support it in the future – benefactors, parliament, government, trustees, staff and visitors.

As always, thanks are due to the Museum's curators, without whose specialised scholarship books such as this could not be produced. Their published works have been heavily drawn upon and their assistance in checking the text is gratefully acknowledged.

Special thanks are due to the editor Laura Brockbank and picture researcher Beatriz Waters for what is very much a team effort. Their advice and practical assistance have been invaluable. The imagination and flair of the designers Sam Blok and Simon Esterson is much appreciated.

The support of Alasdair Macleod, Teresa Francis and British Museum Press is also gratefully acknowledged.

Many members of staff have helped, but the assistance of archivists Christopher Date and Gary Thorn, with their encyclopaedic knowledge of the Museum's history and sources, requires particular mention, as also does the support of the Central Librarian Joanna Bowring. The majority of the photographs have been provided by the Photographic Section.

Finally, thanks are due to Neil MacGregor, Director of the British Museum, for his advice and support.